Diet recommendations during stomach cancer

Diet can support the affected organs and is not a treatment for the disease. Please check these recommendations always with a nutrition consultant, therapist, doctor or dietician. The recipes and the list of ingredients are supporting the conventional medical therapy.
The calorie disclosures of fresh ingredients (fruit and vegetables) vary according to quality and time of harvest. The contents were checked by a dietician and a nutrition consultant for the Traditional Chinese Medicine (TCM).

Author:
©2017 Josef Miligui
www.ebns.at

AF206385

Source:
The lists are created from the EBNS database for nutritional counseling. The database is used by dietitians, therapists and doctors for advising the patient / client.

Literature:
The specialist literature and the training documents of the German and Austrian dietary and traditional Chinese medicine serve as a knowledge base. We have used the documents as a basis of knowledge, adapted it to our experience and completed them.
http://di-book.com

Design:
©2018 Josef Miligui

Production and publishing:
BoD – Books on Demand, Norderstedt
ISBN: 9783746098418

Diet recommendations during stomach cancer

1   Treatment strategy

Smaller but more frequent meals. Reduce fat content of food. Sufficient calorie intake and adequate intake of vitamin B12 and vitamin D as well as calcium. (possibly food supplement)

2   Avoid

Avoid fluid intake with food, lying down after meals. In case of intolerance, avoid dairy products.

3 Breakfast

4 Snack

5 Lunch

6   Afternoon

7   Dinner

8   Any time

9   Recipes

(recommendable) = You can use more.
(little) = You should use less than specified or omit.

9.1   Andalusian fish pot

Strengthens immune system, prevents cancer, dissolves stagnation, promotes weight loss. Good to fight immunodeficiency, loss of appetite, flatulence, high blood pressure, depressions, diabetes, diarrhea, stimulates appetite.
Cooking time approx. 30 min
Calories p. portion: 348
4 portions
Allergens: ADLO

Quantity of ingredients:
Basic recipe for a vegetable soup (nutritious) 2 cups / 500g. (recommended)
Onion (spring onion) 2 pieces / 40g. (yes)
Olive oil 1 table spoon / 20g. (little)
Lemon peel 1/2 piece / 3g. (yes)
Bay leaf 1 piece / 1g. (yes)
Potato 5/8 oz / 200g. (yes)
Cod 3/4 lbs / 300g. (yes)
White wine 4 table spoons / 80g. (little)
Lemon juice 1/2 teaspoon / 10g. (yes)
Salt 1 pinch / 1g. (little)
Pepper (ground) 1 pinch / 0,2g. (yes)
Parsley 1 table spoon / 15g. (recommended)
White bread (wheat bread) 8 slices / 250g. (little)

Cooking instructions:
Boil the vegetable broth with small spring onion, olive oil, grated lemon peel and bay leaf. Boil covered for 10 minutes. Add the peeled, diced potatoes and boil in about 8 minutes. Add fish pieces and white wine and switch to small heat. In the slightly boiling broth put the fish and boil it a few minutes. Season with lemon juice, salt and pepper. Serve with parsley sprinkled.
White bread as a side dish.

9.2   Apple - banana cream

Regulates gastrointestinal function, provides vitamin C, cholesterol lowering, reduces inflammation, diuretic, improves blood circulation.
Cooking time approx. 15 min
Calories p. portion: 110
4 portions
Allergens:

Quantity of ingredients:
Apple (sour) 7/8 lbs / 400g. (recommended)
Water 3/4 cup - 6 oz / 200g. (yes)
Orange peel 1/4 piece / 5g. (yes)
Lemon peel 1/2 piece / 2g. (yes)
Sugar brown 2 teaspoons / 6g. (little)
Cinnamon sticks 1 piece / 0g. (yes)
Banana 1 piece / 150g. (recommended)
Acerola fruit nectar or powder 1 teaspoon / 2g. (recommended)
Orange juice 1/2 piece / 50g. (recommended)
Lemon juice 1 table spoon / 10g. (yes)

Cooking instructions:
Cut the apple into fine slices, bring water to boil and add the apple slices, orange- and lemon peel, sugar and cinnamon and simmer about 7 minutes. The apples should be almost soft. Remove acerola and the cinnamon stick. Mix the apple, the banana, the orange juice and the lemon juice.

9.3   Apricot Oat Balls with Acai powder

Strengthens immune system, little laxative, antioxidativ.
Cooking time approx. 20 min
Calories p. portion: 768
2 portions
Allergens: AHO

Quantity of ingredients:
Oat flakes (whole grain) 1/4 lbs - 4oz / 125g. (recommended)
Apricot dried 1/4 lbs - 4oz / 125g. (recommended)
Almond 1/4 lbs - 4oz / 100g. (little)
Honey 2 table spoons / 14g. (yes)
Acai powder 3 teaspoons / 9g. (recommended)
Lemon juice 2 table spoons / 9g. (yes)

Cooking instructions:
Lightly chop the sliced almonds in the pan and let them cool. Then pour the apricots in the blender and add lemon juice. Mix all the ingredients together. If the mass is too loose add some honey. Finally, form small balls and roll them in oat flakes.

9.4 Avocado with lemon

Good to fight insomnia, inflammation, swelling, pain and itching. Is calming.
Cooking time approx. 5 min
Calories p. portion: 289
1 portions
Allergens:

Quantity of ingredients:
Avocado 1/2 piece / 120g. (recommended)
Lemon juice 1/2 piece / 10g. (yes)
Salt 1 pinch / 1g. (little)

Cooking instructions:
Halve the avocado, remove the core, add the lemon juice, salt a little and eat with a spoon.

9.5 Banana Soymilk

Good to fight loss of appetite, oral mucosa inflammation. Strengthens body energy, promotes stomach-spleen harmony, promotes digestion, regulates gastrointestinal function. Relieves pain, detoxifying, bactericide.
Cooking time approx. 5 min
Calories p. portion: 126
2 portions
Allergens: E

Quantity of ingredients:
Banana 1 piece / 120g. (recommended)
Soybean milk 1 1/2 cups / 400g. (yes)
Honey 1 teaspoon / 3g. (yes)
Cinnamon ground 1 pinch / 1g. (yes)
Acerola fruit nectar or powder 1 teaspoon / 2g. (recommended)

Cooking instructions:
Cut the banana into pieces, puree them with soy milk, acerola, honey and cinnamon with the mixing stick.

9.6   Barley and vegetable soup

Supports urination, detoxifying, promotes spleen and liver, reduces blood pressure, strengthens immune system, prevents cancer, reduces radiation damage, promotes digestion, helps to digest fat, harmonizes metabolism.
Cooking time approx. 2 hours
Calories p. portion: 281
3 portions
Allergens: AGL

Quantity of ingredients:
Barley 1 cup / 120g. (yes)
Shiitake, dried 1/8 oz / 4g. (recommended)
Onion (shallot) 1 piece / 20g. (yes)
Cumin (Caraway seed) 1 knife tip / 0,5g. (yes)
Sunflower oil 1 table spoon / 10g. (little)
Water 1 cup / 250g. (yes)
Celery sticks 2 branches / 20g. (yes)
Peas, green 5/8 lbs - 8oz / 250g. (yes)
Tomato 1 piece / 50g. (yes)
Carrot 2 pieces / 150g. (yes)
French beans Handful / 30g. (yes)
Salt 1 pinch / 1g. (little)
Pepper (ground) 1 pinch / 0,5g. (yes)
Parsley 1 teaspoon / 3g. (recommended)
Butter organic 1 teaspoon / 3g. (little)

Cooking instructions:
Soak the barley in the evening for the next day. Soak the mushrooms separately at the next day. Brown onion and cumin in oil, then boil with water. Add the chopped vegetables, some salt, the barley and the shiitake mushrooms and cook everything to a thick soup. At the end, season with pepper, parsley and a little butter.

9.7 Barley mash with steamed pear

Promotes digestion, supports urination, promotes spleen, diuretic, forcing spleen, relaxes, promotes perspiration.
Cooking time approx. 25 min
Calories p. portion: 114
5 portions
Allergens: A

Quantity of ingredients:
Water 10 cups / 1200g. (yes)
Barley 1 cup / 120g. (yes)
Ginger fresh 2 slices / 2g. (yes)
Cardamom 3 capsules / 1g. (yes)
Salt 1 pinch / 1g. (little)
Pear 1 piece / 200g. (recommended)
Sugar cane sugar 1/2 teaspoon / 5g. (little)

Cooking instructions:
Grind coarse the barley and roast it dry. Add hot water, add ginger and cardamom and let it swell to a pulp in low heat. Peel and dice the pear and boil for 10 minutes with a little water. At the end, add the stewed pear, a little butter and sweetener.

Variant: If you want to go fast, you can use barley flakes instead of shot.

9.8 Basic recipe for a fish broth

Strengthens the kidneys, promotes watering, reduces blood pressure, strengthens immune system, prevents cancer, reduces radiation damage. Low in cholesterol and protein rich. Improves blood circulation, stimulates appetite.
Cooking time approx. 40 min
Calories p. portion: 128
5 portions
Allergens: DLO

Quantity of ingredients:
Fish pieces mixed (fresh water) 3/4 lbs / 300g. (recommended)
Celery root 1/4 lbs - 4oz / 120g. (yes)
Leek 2 inches / 10g. (yes)
Carrot 2 pieces / 150g. (yes)
White wine 1/2 cup / 125g. (little)
Lemon 1/2 piece / 50g. (yes)

Bay leaf 2 leaves / 2g. (yes)
Peppercorns 3 pieces / 2g. (yes)
Olive oil 1 table spoon / 10g. (little)
Water 2 cup / 450g. (yes)

Cooking instructions:
Fry celery, chopped carrots and leeks in olive oil, add bay leaf and peppercorns, add pieces of fish and sauté briefly. Add water, add little white wine or lemon. Simmer gently for 30 minutes. Skim off the resulting foam several times. In the end, sift the ingredients through a cloth.
Refrigerate for later use

9.9   Basic recipe for a reissue soup (Congee)

Low fat content, for the drainage of the body overweight and high blood pressure.
Cooking time approx. 2-4 hours
Calories p. portion: 140
3 portions
Allergens:

Quantity of ingredients:
Rice variety any 1 cup / 120g. (recommended)
Water 6 cups / 700g. (yes)

Cooking instructions:
Cook rice and water in a ratio of about 1: 6. The amount of water determines the thickness of the mash (matter of taste).
Put the rice in a saucepan with a heavy lid. It is important to simmer the rice after a short boil on the slightest flame, otherwise it burns.
Boil the rice for 2-4 hours. The longer he cooks, the more he strengthens.
If you want to eat the dish for breakfast, you can put the rice on just before bedtime.
To be on the safe side, you should first check the behavior of your pot and cooker under observation for a similar amount of time, so that nothing burns.
Refrigerate for later use.

9.10 Basic recipe for a vegetable soup, nutritious

Reduces blood pressure, strengthens immune system, prevents cancer, forcing spleen, dissolves stagnation, promotes weight loss. Good to fight immunodeficiency, high blood pressure, depressions, diabetes, diarrhea, reduces blood lipids.
Cooking time approx. 2-3 hours
Calories p. portion: 48
5 portions
Allergens: L

Quantity of ingredients:
Olive oil 1 table spoon / 4g. (little)
Onion white 1 piece / 60g. (yes)
Carrot 3 pieces / 200g. (yes)
Parsnip 3/8 lbs - 6oz / 150g. (recommended)
Celery root 1 cup / 100g. (yes)
Ginger fresh 1/2 teaspoon / 2g. (yes)
Lemon 1/2 piece / 25g. (yes)
Juniper berry 6 pieces / 6g. (yes)
Thyme dried 1 pinch / 1g. (yes)
Lovage 1 table spoon / 3g. (yes)
Bay leaf 2 leaves / 1g. (yes)
Salt 1 pinch / 1g. (little)
Water 3 cups / 650g. (yes)

Cooking instructions:
Cut the vegetables into cubes.
Heat oil in hot pot, fry shortly onions and vegetables.
Add cold water, then add ginger, bay leaf and lemon juice.
Season with juniper, thyme and lovage. Cover for 2 - 3 hours on a low heat and simmer.
The used vegetables should be thrown away.
The basic recipe serves as a soup base and to refine vegetables, legumes or cereals.
If you want to eat vegetable soup immediately, add the desired vegetables half an hour before.
Refrigerate for later use.

9.11 Basmati rice + Zucchini tofu dish

Diuretic, supports urination, harmonizes spleen and stomach, reduces flatulence, good to fight body overweight and high blood pressure. Antioxidativ, promotes digestion, perspiration, reduces blood lipids, forcing spleen.
Cooking time approx. 20 min
Calories p. portion: 146
4 portions
Allergens: E

Quantity of ingredients:
Soy Tofu 5/8 lbs - 8oz / 250g. (yes)
Olive oil 2 table spoons / 6g. (little)
Coriander 1/2 teaspoon / 4g. (yes)
Ginger fresh 1/2 teaspoon / 4g. (yes)
Rice Basmati 1/2 cup / 60g. (recommended)
Water 3 cups / 200g. (yes)
Zucchini 1 piece / 700g. (yes)

Cooking instructions:
Cut tofu cubes and marinate with olive oil, tamari, crushed coriander and ginger. Leave at least 1 hour.

Cook Basmati rice with the water. You can season with onion and cardamom.
Roast zucchini and tofu in pan in the hot oil for approx. 5-7 min.
Serve rice and tofu on a plate.
Add the parsley.

Can also be used as a salad for the home and on the go.

9.12 Bean paste piquant sweet

Supports urination, lowers cholesterol, prevents arteriosclerosis, antioxidativ. Promotes digestion, helps to digest fat, supports urination, reduces blood pressure.
Cooking time approx. 1 hour
Calories p. portion: 311
1 portions
Allergens: MO

Quantity of ingredients:
Black beans 1 cup / 120g. (recommended)
Ginger fresh 1 inch / 3g. (yes)
Boxhorn clover seeds 1/2 teaspoon / 2g. (yes)
Tomato paste 1 table spoon / 10g. (recommended)
Olive oil 2 table spoons / 20g. (little)
Pumpkin seed oil 1 dash / 3g. (little)
Mustard 1 knife tip / 1g. (yes)
Radish horseradish 1 teaspoon (grated) / 2g. (yes)
Pepper (ground) 1 pinch / 0,5g. (yes)
Garlic 2 cloves / 3g. (recommended)
Salt 1 pinch / 1g. (little)
Sugar molasses 2 table spoons / 20g. (little)
Lemon peel 1/2 piece / 1g. (yes)

Cooking instructions:
Boil beans (with spices and ginger), drain water and puree. Season with spices.

Refine with sugar beet syrup and lemon peel.

9.13 Beluga lentil stew with vegetables

Promotes sweating, dissolves stagnation. Relieves constipation, strengthens mother milk production, stimulates nerves, detoxifying, reduces inflammation, improves blood circulation. Strengthens heart and kidney, diuretic, calms the stomach, promotes digestion.
Cooking time approx. 20 min
Calories p. portion: 201
5 portions
Allergens:

Quantity of ingredients:
Lentils 1 1/2 cups / 240g. (yes)
Water 4-5 cups / 500g. (yes)
Carrot 3 pieces / 150g. (yes)
Leek 1 piece / 300g. (yes)
Kohlrabi 1/2 piece / 200g. (recommended)
Tomato 2 pieces / 80g. (yes)
Onion white 1 piece / 50g. (yes)
Bay leaf 2 leaves / 1g. (yes)
Fennel 1 piece / 250g. (recommended)
Star anise 2 pieces / 1g. (yes)

Juniper berry 6 pieces / 2g. (yes)
Olive oil 2 table spoons / 30g. (little)
Salt 1 pinch / 1g. (little)
Ginger fresh 1/2 teaspoon / 2g. (yes)
Black caraway 1 pinch / 1g. (yes)

Cooking instructions:
Heat oil in hot pot. Fry onions and add diced vegetables and spices, lentils (washed well) and salt. Cover with cold water (3 fingers wide) and cook for 20 minutes on a low heat.
Sprinkle with fresh herbs and black cumin

Goes well with rice!

9.14 Bircher-muesli with yogurt, nuts and apple

Fibre-rich, relieves constipation, strengthens immune system, forcing spleen, promotes weight loss. Good to fight immunodeficiency, loss of appetite.
Cooking time approx. 2 hours and more
Calories p. portion: 383
1 portions
Allergens: AGH

Quantity of ingredients:
Muesli 2 table spoons / 20g. (yes)
Oat flakes (whole grain) 2 table spoons / 20g. (recommended)
Yogurt (natural, 3.5% fat) 6 table spoons / 80g. (little)
Lemon 1 table spoon / 10g. (yes)
Acerola fruit nectar or powder 1/2 teaspoon / 1g. (recommended)
Apple (sour) 1 piece / 170g. (recommended)
Hazelnuts 1 table spoon / 10g. (little)

Cooking instructions:
Soak oatmeal in the yogurt for several hours in the fridge. Add rubed nuts, lemon juice, acerola, grated apple. For sweets, raisins can be used.

9.15 Breakfast - Rice with fruits

Good to fight blood circulation disorders, thrombose, risk of embolism, high blood pressure, a headache, heart attack and stroke. Encourages blood build-up, promotes digestion, reduces Inflammation.
Cooking time approx. 10 min - 3 hours
Calories p. portion: 231
3 portions
Allergens: GHO

Quantity of ingredients:
Basic recipe for a rice soup (Congee) 6 cups / 500g. (recommended)
Cow's milk (whole milk 3.5% fat) 1/2 to 1 cup / 80g. (little)
Honey 1 table spoon / 10g. (yes)
Butter organic 1 table spoon / 15g. (little)
Dates dried 1 table spoon / 15g. (recommended)
Fig 1 table spoon / 15g. (yes)
Apple (sour) 1 piece / 200g. (recommended)
Hazelnuts 1/2 teaspoon / 5g. (little)
Almond 1/2 teaspoon / 5g. (little)
Cinnamon ground 1 pinch / 1g. (yes)

Cooking instructions:
Cook rice congee according to basic recipe or use pre-cooked.
Make it with the milk more fluid and sweet with honey.
Fry the fruits and nuts in butter and mix with the finished rice soup, add chopped dates, figs and the apple.

9.16 Broccoli cream soup

Strengthen your immune system, build and maintain healthy bones, teeth, hair and nails. Reduces blood pressure, strengthens immune system, prevents cancer, reduces radiation damage.
Cooking time approx. 30 min
Calories p. portion: 98
6 portions
Allergens: LO

Quantity of ingredients:
Olive oil 2 table spoons / 7g. (little)
Broccoli 1,1 lbs / 500g. (yes)
Carrot 2 pieces / 150g. (yes)
Potato 2 pieces / 120g. (yes)
Onion white 1 piece / 50g. (yes)

Water 1 cup / 50g. (yes)
Basic recipe for a vegetable soup (nutritious) 2 cup / 500g. (recommended)
White wine 1/2 cup / 125g. (little)
Sage 1 teaspoon / 2g. (yes)
Rosemary 1 teaspoon / 2g. (yes)
Pepper (ground) 1 pinch / 0,5g. (yes)
Salt 1 pinch / 1g. (little)

Cooking instructions:
Add the olive oil to the pan, add the washed and cut broccoli, diced carrots and potatoes, sauté for a short time, add the chopped onion, fill with water, enough water to cover the vegetables at least 3 finger breadths. Add bouillon, salt, add a little bit of white wine, add the seasoned sage and rosemary.
Heat till it boils and then simmer on a small fire for about 25 minutes.
Season with pepper, if necessary season with sea salt. Purée the soup.

9.17 Carrot and potato rucola sandwich

Reduces inflammation, improves digestion, supports urination, lowers cholesterol, strengthens immune system, prevents cancer, good to fight constipation (Fibre-rich), dissolves stagnation.
Cooking time approx. 20 min
Calories p. portion: 94
4 portions
Allergens: AG

Quantity of ingredients:
Potato (mealy) 5/8 oz / 200g. (yes)
Carrot 1 piece / 50g. (yes)
Sour cream 15% fat 2 table spoons / 45g. (little)
Onion (spring onion) 1 piece / 20g. (yes)
Rucola 1/2 bunch / 100g. (yes)
Lemon peel 1/4 teaspoon / 1g. (yes)
Salt 1 pinch / 1g. (little)
Pepper (ground) 1 pinch / 0,2g. (yes)
Whole grain bread 8 slices / 48g. (recommended)

Cooking instructions:
Cook the potatoes gently, peel and squeeze through the potato press.
Cook vegetable broth according to the basic recipe and remove a carrot after a short cooking time and finely crush with a fork.

Stir the potatoes, carrots, grated lemon zest and sour cream into a smooth cream.

Mix carrot and potato cream with finely chopped rocket salad. Season the spread with salt and pepper and spread the bread. Sprinkle with the finely chopped young onions.

9.18 Carrot and rice gruel soup

Stops diarrhea, good to fight fever, strengthens immune system, reduces blood pressure.
Cooking time approx. 10 min
Calories p. portion: 101
1 portions
Allergens:

Quantity of ingredients:
Basic recipe for a rice soup (Congee) 1 cup / 120g. (recommended)
Carrot 2 pieces / 100g. (yes)
Salt 1 teaspoon / 4g. (little)

Cooking instructions:
Peel and grate carrots. Heat the rice soup (according to the basic recipe) till it boils and add the grated carrots and salt. Cook for 10 minutes.

9.19 Carrot Risotto

Strengthens immune system, prevents cancer, loss of appetite, flatulence, high blood pressure, depressions, diabetes, diarrhea, stimulates liver function, dissolves stagnation.
Cooking time approx. 45 min
Calories p. portion: 308
2 portions
Allergens: GL

Quantity of ingredients:
Olive oil 1/2 teaspoon / 5g. (little)
Onion (spring onion) 2 table spoons / 7g. (yes)
Nutmeg 1 pinch / 0,3g. (yes)
Parsley 1/2 bunch / 25g. (recommended)
Rice variety any 1/4 lbs - 4oz / 100g. (recommended)
Carrot 5/8 lbs - 8oz / 250g. (yes)
Basic recipe for a vegetable soup (nutritious) 1 cup / 280g. (recommended)

Fennel seeds ground 1/4 teaspoon / 1g. (yes)
Basil (fresh) 1/2 teaspoon / 2g. (yes)
Salt 1 pinch / 1g. (little)
Pepper (ground) 1 pinch / 0,3g. (yes)
Parmesan 1 table spoon / 10g. (little)

Cooking instructions:
Heat the oil in a pan, fry the onions in a glassy and very soft manner.
Add parsley, sauté briefly. Add rice, carrots and nutmeg, sauté briefly
while stirring. Add the vegetable stock, season with fennel and basil,
heat till it boils and cook for about 20 minutes until the rice and carrots
are well. Stir from time to time and add some vegetable stock if
necessary. The risotto should be slightly soupy. Just before the end of
the cooking time mix in the white wine and simmer the risotto for a short
while. Remove risotto from the heat, mix in Parmesan.

9.20 Chicken soup with green spelt, parsley and sake

Strengthens blood, strengthens bone marrow, reduces blood pressure,
strengthens immune system, stimulates liver function, detoxifying.
Improves blood circulation, improves medication effect, stimulates
appetite.
Cooking time approx. 1 1/2 hours
Calories p. portion: 150
2 portions
Allergens: AL

Quantity of ingredients:
Basic recipe for a chicken soup (warming) 2 cup / 500g.
(recommended)
Green spelt 4 table spoons / 30g. (recommended)
Parsley 2 table spoons / 14g. (recommended)
Sake 1 dash / 2g. (yes)

Cooking instructions:
Cook the chicken broth according to the basic recipe. Add the
ingredients in the soup and simmer 10 min.

9.21 Colorful rice dish

Strengthens immune system, good to fight diabetes, strengthens spleen and stomach, strengthens blood, strengthens the muscles, tendons and bones, promotes digestion, helps to digest fat, supports urination, reduces blood pressure, dissolves stagnation.
Cooking time approx. 45 min
Calories p. portion: 437
3 portions
Allergens: L

Quantity of ingredients:
Olive oil 2 teaspoons / 20g. (little)
Onion (spring onion) 1 piece / 20g. (yes)
Beef meat 1/4 lbs - 4oz / 125g. (yes)
Rice (whole grain) 3 oz / 80g. (recommended)
Basic recipe for a vegetable soup (nutritious) 1 cup / 300g. (recommended)
Celery root 1/8 lbs - 2oz / 50g. (yes)
Leek 1 piece / 100g. (yes)
Beans (green, fresh) 3/8 lbs - 6oz / 150g. (yes)
Carrot 1 piece / 70g. (yes)
Tomato 2 pieces / 100g. (yes)
Salt 1 pinch / 0,5g. (little)
Pepper (ground) 1 pinch / 0,2g. (yes)
Peppers powder 1 pinch / 0,5g. (yes)
Herbs various 2 table spoons / 12g. (yes)

Cooking instructions:
Wash leek and carrots, clean and chop them. Dice the celery, slice the tomatoes.

Fry in a large, deep pan with oil, onion and minced meat.

Add brown rice and prepared vegetables (celery, leeks, beans, carrots, tomatoes). Braise briefly.

Season with salt, pepper and paprika. Add vegetable broth. Heat till it boils and cook over low heat for 20 to 30 minutes with the lid closed.

Sprinkle with fresh chopped herbs and serve.

9.22 Compote from apples

Apple (sweet) stops diarrhea, promotes digestion, appetizing, harmonizes the stomach. Warms stomach and spleen, improves blood circulation.
Cooking time approx. 10 min
Calories p. portion: 67
2 portions
Allergens:

Quantity of ingredients:
Apple (sweet) 1 piece / 220g. (recommended)
Water 1 1/2 cups / 220g. (yes)
Cinnamon ground 1 pinch / 1g. (yes)

Cooking instructions:
Cook the apples (organic) with the skin and seeds. Sprinkle with cinnamon.

9.23 Couscous Salad

prevents cancer, forcing spleen, promotes digestion, stimulates liver function, reduces blood pressure, strengthens immune system, reduces radiation damage, diuretic.
Cooking time approx. 25 min
Calories p. portion: 338
3 portions
Allergens: A

Quantity of ingredients:
Water 1 cup / 100g. (yes)
Olive oil 1 table spoon / 15g. (little)
Couscous 5/8 oz / 200g. (yes)
Lemon juice 2 table spoons / 30g. (yes)
Lemon peel 1 teaspoon / 2g. (yes)
Tomato 2 pieces / 80g. (yes)
Cucumber 1/4 lbs - 4oz / 100g. (yes)
Carrot 1/4 lbs - 4oz / 100g. (yes)
Parsley 1 Bunch / 100g. (recommended)
Chives 1 Bunch / 100g. (yes)
Peppermint 3 twigs / 30g. (yes)

Cooking instructions:
Boil in a small saucepan 250 ml. water with salt and 1 tablespoon olive oil. Add the couscous, take the stove in the front and let it swell covered for 5 minutes. Put the couscous back on the stove and let it simmer for about 2 minutes with gentle stirring. If necessary, add 1 - 3 tbsp of hot water.
Mix the couscous with lemon juice, chopped lemon peel and 1 tbsp oil, season with salt and pepper and leave to set.
Add couscous with tomatoes, cucumber, parsley (all diced), carrots (grated), chives and mint (finely chopped). Season the couscous salad with lemon juice, salt and pepper.

9.24 Cous-Cous with date, coco and almondpuree

Stops diarrhea, promotes digestion, appetizing, relieves diarrhea.
Cooking time approx. 10 min
Calories p. portion: 484
3 portions
Allergens: AHO

Quantity of ingredients:
Couscous 1 1/2 cups / 240g. (yes)
Water 4 cups / 400g. (yes)
Dates dried 6 pieces / 20g. (recommended)
Coconut flakes 2 table spoons / 30g. (little)
Almond puree 2 table spoons / 20g. (little)
Olive oil 2 teaspoons / 20g. (little)
Apple (sweet) 1 piece grated / 120g. (recommended)
Vanilla 1 knife tip / 0,2g. (yes)

Cooking instructions:
Put couscous and olive oil in a large bowl and pour boiling water over them. Let it swell for 10 minutes. Crush dates and grate apple. Loosen up cous-cous with a fork. Mix in dates, coconut flakes, apple and almond paste.
Sweet to taste. Spices and flavors: vanilla, little chili

Winter variation: pear,
Summer variation: apricot, nectarine

9.25 Cranberry juice

Antibacterial, good to fight loss of appetite, arteriosclerosis, bladder infections, diarrhea, colds. Antipyretic, against free radicals, gout, diuretic, stomach ulcers, oral mucosa inflammation, rheumatism.
Cooking time approx. 5 min
Calories p. portion: 43
1 portions
Allergens:

Quantity of ingredients:
Cranberries 2 table spoons / 25g. (recommended)
Water 1 cup / 125g. (yes)
Honey 1 table spoon / 10g. (yes)

Cooking instructions:
Mix the cranberries with a little water with the blender to a pulp. Add the remaining water and sweeten with the honey.

9.26 Cream cheese substitute

Good to fight lactose intolerance. Strengthens body energy, promotes digestion, promotes weight loss. Good to fight immunodeficiency, loss of appetite, arteriosclerosis, flatulence, bladder weakness, anemia, high blood pressure, depressions, diabetes, diarrhea.
Cooking time approx. 20 min
Calories p. portion: 526
2 portions
Allergens: AE

Quantity of ingredients:
Soybean milk 4 cup / 300g. (yes)
Lemon 1 piece / 50g. (yes)
Herbs various 2 table spoons / 6g. (yes)
Whole grain bread 6 slices / 300g. (recommended)

Cooking instructions:
Heat the soy milk in a saucepan till it boils, stirring occasionally (gets burn easily!), Then allow to cool.
Squeeze out the lemon and stir gently under the cooled soy milk (approx. 80°C/176°F), let it approx. 20 min. rest or clot.
Pour chopped soy milk through a strainer lined with a dishcloth, allow liquid to drain and then squeeze out remaining liquid with the dishcloth. Refine to taste with fresh herbs. Serve with wholemeal bread.

9.27 Delicately spiced zucchini with tomatoes

Diuretic, promotes digestion, helps to digest fat, reduces blood pressure, dissolves stagnation, antioxidativ, supports urination, diuretic, warming the body from the inside, expands blood vessels.
Cooking time approx. 10 min
Calories p. portion: 203
4 portions
Allergens:

Quantity of ingredients:
Olive oil 1 table spoon / 20g. (little)
Onion white 2 pieces / 120g. (yes)
Zucchini 4 pieces / 800g. (yes)
Oregano dried 1 pinch / 1g. (yes)
Basil (fresh) 6-8 leaves / 3g. (yes)
Salt 1 pinch / 1g. (little)
Tomato 2 pieces / 120g. (yes)
Rice (whole grain) 1 cup / 120g. (recommended)
Water 6 cups / 400g. (yes)
Salt 1 pinch / 1g. (little)

Cooking instructions:
In a hot pan, fry olive oil, finely chopped onions and finely chopped zucchini until half cooked. Add plenty of dried oregano. Salt and chop the tomatoes for a few minutes until the zucchini are tender but crisp. Add fresh basil as desired.

Variation: Put some sheep's cheese over the tomatoes and finish cooking with the lid closed.

Place the rice in salted water, heat till it boils and let it simmer over low heat for about 15 minutes.

9.28 Exotic lenses

Strengthens heart and kidney, diuretic, dalms the stomach, promotes digestion, dissolves stagnation, helps to digest fat, supports urination, reduces blood pressure, detoxifying and stimulating the immune system.
Cooking time approx. 45 min
Calories p. portion: 144
4 portions
Allergens: NO

Quantity of ingredients:
Sesame oil 1 table spoon / 10g. (little)
Onion white 2 pieces / 120g. (yes)
Ginger fresh 1/2 teaspoon / 2g. (yes)
Thyme dried 1/2 teaspoon / 1g. (yes)
Cumin (Caraway seed) 1/2 teaspoon / 2g. (yes)
Lentils red 1 cup / 120g. (yes)
Wakame 1 inch / 1g. (yes)
Lemon 1/2 piece / 20g. (yes)
Bocksdorn fruits (Fructus Lycii, goji berry dried 2 pinches / 2g. (yes)
Sugar cane sugar 1 pinch / 1g. (little)
Salt 1 pinch / 1g. (little)
Vinegar (Apple vinegar) 1/2 teaspoon / 1g. (yes)
Tomato 1 piece / 50g. (yes)
Chard 5/8 oz / 200g. (yes)
Cauliflower 5/8 oz / 200g. (recommended)
Salt 1 pinch / 1g. (little)
Rice (whole grain) 1/2 cup / 60g. (recommended)
Water 3 cups / 300g. (yes)
Salt 1 pinch / 1g. (little)

Cooking instructions:
Heat sesame oil in a hot pot. Add chopped onions, grated ginger, dried thyme, plenty of cumin and sauté gently. Add peeled red lentils, a strip of wakame, a little lemon juice, hot water and some dried buckthorn fruits. Simmer for 20 minutes until the lentils are cooked; add hot water as needed to make a pulp. Add sugar, some chili and salt. Add vinegar or lemon juice depending on your taste. Add chopped tomatoes as desired. Let it pass for a few minutes.

Cook in a small pot with 1 cup of water and a little salt the cauliflower 10 min. until soft.
Blanch in a small pot with 1 cup of water and salt the chard 3 min.

Boil the rice briefly, salt and 10 min. to let go. Serve everything with the lentil dish.

9.29 Fast polenta with avocado and spring onion

Good to fight inflammations, swelling, pain. Forcing spleen and stomach, lets urine and bile juice flow, dissolves stagnation. Includes unsaturated fatty acids, antioxidativ.
Cooking time approx. 10 min
Calories p. portion: 450
2 portions
Allergens:

Quantity of ingredients:
Corn (fast polenta) 1 cup / 120g. (yes)
Water 1 1/2 cups / 240g. (yes)
Olive oil 1 table spoon / 15g. (little)
Salt 1 pinch / 1g. (little)
Pepper (ground) 1 pinch / 0,5g. (yes)
Lemon juice 1 dash / 3g. (yes)
Onion (spring onion) 2 pieces / 40g. (yes)
Avocado 1/2 piece / 150g. (recommended)
Turmeric (yellow root) 1 pinch / 1g. (recommended)
Basil (fresh) 1 teaspoon / 2g. (yes)

Cooking instructions:
Heat water, add oil, lemon and spices.
When the water boils, add the polenta while stirring constantly and cook for 2 minutes.
When the porridge becomes firm, the polenta is ready.
Add diced avocado and sliced spring onion to the polenta. Sprinkle fresh basil on it.

9.30 Fennel-Rice Soup

Forcing spleen, relieves constipation, stimulates nerves, detoxifying, reduces inflammation, improves blood circulation.
Cooking time approx. 15-20 min
Calories p. portion: 156
2 portions
Allergens: EG

Quantity of ingredients:
Basic recipe for a rice soup (Congee) 1 cup / 300g. (recommended)
Fennel 1/2 piece / 150g. (recommended)
Butter organic 1 table spoon / 15g. (little)
Soy sauce 1 dash / 3g. (little)

Cooking instructions:
Cook the fennel softly in the rice soup according to the basic recipe.
Before serving, add a piece of butter and some soy sauce.

9.31 Fine Russian borscht

Strengths spleen and stomach, strengthens the heart, stimulates digestion, reduces blood pressure, strengthens immune system. For strengthening after diseases. Good to fight bloating, cramping in gastrointestinal complaints.
Cooking time approx. 30 min
Calories p. portion: 172
6 portions
Allergens: AGLO

Quantity of ingredients:
Red beet 5/8 oz / 200g. (yes)
Sunflower oil 1 table spoon / 10g. (little)
Onion (shallot) 2 pieces / 40g. (yes)
Carrot 2 pieces / 140g. (yes)
Celery root 1 piece / 500g. (yes)
Parsley root 1 piece / 150g. (yes)
Leek 1/8 lbs - 2oz / 50g. (yes)
Basic recipe for a vegetable soup (nutritious) 3 cups / 650g. (recommended)
Bay leaf 1 Leaf / 0,2g. (yes)
Juniper berry 2 pieces / 2g. (yes)
Nutmeg 1 pinch / 1g. (yes)
Savoy cabbage / kale 5/8 oz / 200g. (yes)
Salt 1 pinch / 1g. (little)
Pepper (ground) 1 pinch / 0,5g. (yes)
Ground 1 pinch / 1g. (yes)
Red wine 1/2 cup / 125g. (little)
Sour cream 15% fat 1 table spoon / 10g. (little)
Dill 1 teaspoon / 10g. (recommended)
White bread (wheat bread) 6 slices / 120g. (little)

Cooking instructions:
Fry some beetroot in oil. Fry the onions, carrots, celery, parsley root and leek well in another pan. Add the stock and the wine; then add bay leaves, juniper berries and nutmeg and simmer for 15 minutes. Remove the bay leaf and puree everything.

Heat more broth separately, simmer the steamed beetroot in it. Add cabbage or white cabbage after half the cooking time and let it steep. At the end, add the pureed vegetables and season with salt, pepper, ground cumin and a little red wine. Garnish with some sour cream and finely chopped dill in the plate. Serve with a slice of white bread.

9.32 Fish soup with rosemary

Promotes spleen and liver, reduces blood pressure, strengthens immune system, prevents cancer, reduces radiation damage, has little cholesterol and is protein rich, improves blood circulation, increases appetite. Antioxidant, forcing spleen, dissolves stagnation.
Cooking time approx. 30 min
Calories p. portion: 271
4 portions
Allergens: DLO

Quantity of ingredients:
Basic recipe for a fish soup 2 cup / 500g. (yes)
Rosemary 1/2 bunch / 7g. (yes)
Onion (spring onion) 1 piece / 20g. (yes)
Olive oil 2 table spoons / 35g. (little)
Fish pieces mixed (fresh water) 5/8 lbs - 8oz / 250g. (recommended)
Carrot 1 piece / 120g. (yes)
Parsnip 1 piece / 180g. (recommended)
Celery root 1 slice / 20g. (yes)
Salt 1 pinch / 1g. (little)
Peppercorns 2 pieces / 1g. (yes)
Garlic 1 clove / 3g. (recommended)

Cooking instructions:
Fry the onion and garlic in oil. Add fish broth. Add diced carrots, parsnips and celery. Season with salt and peppercorns. Simmer the soup on a low heat for 25 minutes.
Wash the fish, drizzle with lemon juice, divide into pieces and add to the soup with the pink rosemary. Cook for 5 min on low heat.
Add the chives and parsley and season the soup with the salt.

9.33 Grated apple

Eat 3 times a day - Apple (sour) scraped and brown is stuffing. Relieves diarrhea.
Cooking time approx. 10 min
Calories p. portion: 120
1 portions
Allergens:
Quantity of ingredients:
Apple (sour) 1 piece / 200g. (recommended)

Cooking instructions:
Peel apple and grate as fine as possible. Leave for at least 5 minutes until it turns brown.

9.34 Halibut with tomato and garlic sauce

Promotes digestion, helps to digest fat, supports urination, reduces blood pressure, good to fight rheumatism, flatulence, bladder weakness, anemia, high blood pressure, depressions, diabetes, diarrhea. Valuable omega-3 fatty acids.
Cooking time approx. 45 min
Calories p. portion: 319
5 portions
Allergens: D

Quantity of ingredients:
Rice variety any 1 cup / 120g. (recommended)
Water 6 cups / 240g. (yes)
Salt 1 pinch / 1g. (little)
Halibut (Flatfish) 2,2 lbs / 800g. (yes)
Salt 1 pinch / 1g. (little)
Pepper (ground) 1 pinch / 0,5g. (yes)
Lemon juice 1 dach / 2g. (yes)
Bay leaf 2 pieces / 2g. (yes)
Lemon 1 piece / 30g. (yes)
Garlic 8 pieces / 10g. (recommended)
Thyme dried 1 table spoon / 5g. (yes)
Olives 0,2 lbs / 75g. (little)
Tomato 4 pieces / 200g. (yes)
Salt 1 pinch / 1g. (little)
Pepper (ground) 1 pinch / 0,5g. (yes)

Cooking instructions:
Cook rice with salted water (1:3).
Rinse the fish under running cold water, dab with kitchen paper and rub with salt, pepper and lemon juice.
Place the fish fillets in a casserole dish with pieces of bay leaf.

Wash the lemon hot and cut into slices, peel and halve the garlic.
Sprinkle the olives and the thyme over them.
Brew the tomatoes with hot water, skin and chop.

Mix all ingredients, season with salt and pepper and distribute around the fish.

Cook everything at 200°C/392°F for about 20 minutes.
Serve with the rice.

9.35 Japanese algae soup

Reduces blood pressure, strengthens immune system, prevents cancer, reduces radiation damage. Promotes digestion. Detoxifying and stimulates the immune system.
Cooking time approx. 20 min
Calories p. portion: 47
3 portions
Allergens:

Quantity of ingredients:
Wakame 1 oz / 25g. (yes)
Water 2 cup / 450g. (yes)
Onion (shallot) 1-2 pcs. / 30g. (yes)
Radish (white, green, purple-red) 1/8 lbs - 2oz / 50g. (yes)
Carrot 2 pieces / 180g. (yes)
Miso 2 table spoons / 20g. (yes)
Parsley 2 table spoons / 20g. (recommended)
Onion (spring onion) 1 table spoon (sliced)

Cooking instructions:
Soak wakame in water for a few minutes, remove and bring the water to the boil. Add finely chopped onions and wakame, radishes and carrots, cut into thin strips, and simmer for another 10 minutes. Dissolve miso in a little cooled cooking water and add it at the end. Sprinkle with parsley and spring onions.

9.36 Kohlrabi in chervil sauce with potatoes

Reduces inflammation, lowers cholesterol, diuretic, conducts bowel winds, strengthens immune system, prevents cancer, promotes weight loss. Good to fight loss of appetite, flatulence, high blood pressure, depressions, diabetes, diarrhea.
Cooking time approx. 1 hour
Calories p. portion: 188
4 portions
Allergens: GL

Quantity of ingredients:
Potato 6 pieces / 450g. (yes)
Basic recipe for a vegetable soup (nutritious) 1 cup / 300g. (recommended)
Potato 1/4 lbs - 4oz / 100g. (yes)
Nutmeg 1 pinch / 0,2g. (yes)
Lemon peel 1/2 teaspoon / 2g. (yes)
Ginger fresh 1/2 teaspoon / 2g. (yes)
Lovage 1/2 teaspoon / 2g. (yes)
Kohlrabi 3/4 lbs / 300g. (recommended)
Salt 1 pinch / 1g. (little)
Pepper (ground) 1 pinch / 0,2g. (yes)
Sour cream 15% fat 2 table spoons / 30g. (little)
Chervil dried 1 Bunch / 80g. (recommended)

Cooking instructions:
Boil the potatoes in salted water.
Bring half of the vegetable stock to boil. Add the diced potatoes, nutmeg, lemon zest, ginger and lovage. Cover the potatoes and cook for about 10 minutes until soft and puree them with a blender until they are smooth.
Bring remaining vegetable stock to boil. Cut kohlrabi into cubes and add, cover and cook for about 8 minutes. Stir in the potato sauce and heat everything briefly.
Puree with the mixing stick chervil and sour cream. Mix the chervil cream with the kohlrabi vegetables.
Serve with the cooked, peeled potatoes.

9.37 Lettuce with fresh cheese

The bitter substances have diuretic effect and promote the blood circulation in the digestive area. Mustard improves thyroid function, relieves rheumatism symptoms.
Cooking time approx. 5 min
Calories p. portion: 802
1 portions
Allergens: AFM

Quantity of ingredients:
Leaf salads (bitter) 2 portions / 60g. (recommended)
Fresh cheese from soya 3/8 lbs - 6oz / 150g. (yes)
Mustard 1 knife tip / 1g. (yes)
Lemon juice 1 dash / 3g. (yes)
Salt 1 pinch / 1g. (little)
Pepper (ground) 1 pinch / 0,5g. (yes)
Herbs various 2 teaspoons / 4g. (yes)
Black caraway 1 pinch / 1g. (yes)
Whole grain bread 2 slices / 40g. (recommended)

Cooking instructions:
Wash lettuce and finely pluck.
Mix 150 ml cream cheese, splashes of mustard, splashes of lemon juice, 1 clove of garlic, chopped fresh herbs, pinch of pepper and crushed black cumin and pour over. Serve with wholemeal bread.

9.38 Marinated courgette with smoked tofu

Diuretic, reduces flatulence, good to fight chronic diarrhea, stomach bleeding, improves digestion, relaxing and reassuring.
Cooking time approx. 30 min
Calories p. portion: 132
2 portions
Allergens: EL

Quantity of ingredients:
Zucchini 7/8 lbs / 400g. (yes)
Salt 1 pinch / 1g. (little)
Lemon juice 2 table spoons / 15g. (yes)
Basic recipe for a vegetable soup (nutritious) 2 table spoons / 30g. (recommended)
Olive oil 1 table spoon / 10g. (little)
Basil 2 table spoons / 10g. (yes)

Oregano fresh 1/2 teaspoon / 2g. (yes)
Peppermint 1 teaspoon / 4g. (yes)
Capers in olive oil 1 table spoon / 8g. (yes)
Lemon peel 1/2 teaspoon / 2g. (yes)
Soy Tofu smoked 1/4 lbs - 4oz / 100g. (yes)

Cooking instructions:
Preheat the oven to 200°C/392°F (circulating air 180°C/356°F).
Cover a baking tray with baking paper and place the zucchini next to
each other. Cook zucchini in preheated oven for 5 minutes, turn over
and cook for another 5-6 minutes.

Mix the lemon juice, vegetable stock and oil with the whisk. Stir in basil,
oregano, mint, chopped capers and grated lemon peel. Season the
marinade with salt.

Mix the hot zucchini with the marinade and let cool.

Arrange marinated zucchini with smoked tofu cubes.

9.39 Millet with shiitake mushrooms and avocado

Anti-inflammatory, good to fight swelling and pain, promotes spleen
and kidney, diuretic, stimulates digestion, building up, eye-enhancing,
detoxifying, nerve-strengthening, building up.
Cooking time approx. 20 min
Calories p. portion: 560
2 portions
Allergens: G

Quantity of ingredients:
Millet 1 cup / 120g. (recommended)
Water 1 1/2 cups / 200g. (yes)
Shiitake, dried 1 oz / 25g. (recommended)
Ginger fresh 1/2 teaspoon / 2g. (yes)
Pepper (ground) 1 pinch / 0,5g. (yes)
Salt 1 pinch / 1g. (little)
Parsley 1 table spoon / 7g. (recommended)
Peppers powder 1 pinch / 1g. (yes)
Butter organic 1 table spoon / 15g. (little)
Avocado 1 piece / 200g. (recommended)
Lemon juice 1 dash / 3g. (yes)
Rucola 2 handful / 30g. (yes)

Cooking instructions:
In a saucepan with hot water, sprinkle the millet, add in strips cut shiitake mushrooms and some ginger and simmer; add a pinch of ground pepper, a little salt, plenty of parsley, a pinch of rose pepper, stir in a piece of butter.
In the meantime: place ½ peeled avocado per serving on one half of the plate: sprinkle with a little ground pepper, a small pinch of salt; drizzle with lemon juice; sprinkle a little chopped rocket or rose paprika over it. Put the millet dish on the other half of the plate.

9.40 Muesli with Acai Powder

Fibre-rich, relieves constipation, strengthens immune system, digestive-regulating, forcing spleen, promotes weight loss. Good to fight immunodeficiency, loss of appetite.
Cooking time approx. 2 hours and more
Calories p. portion: 391
1 portions
Allergens: AGH

Quantity of ingredients:
Muesli 2 table spoons / 20g. (yes)
Oat flakes (whole grain) 2 table spoons / 20g. (recommended)
Yogurt (natural, 3.5% fat) 6 table spoons / 80g. (little)
Lemon 1 table spoon / 10g. (yes)
Acerola fruit nectar or powder 1/2 teaspoon / 1g. (recommended)
Acai powder 1 teaspoon / 2g. (recommended)
Apple (sour) 1 piece / 170g. (recommended)
Hazelnuts 1 table spoon / 10g. (little)

Cooking instructions:
Soak oatmeal in the yogurt for several hours in the fridge. Grate nuts, add lemon juice, acerola and acai powder, grated apple. For sweets, raisins can be used.

9.41 Noodles with turkeymeat and pineapple

Solves bile-, kidney- and bladder stones, provides Vitamin C, strengthens blood, strengthens bone marrow, reduces inflammation, supports urination.
Cooking time approx. 45 min
Calories p. portion: 292
4 portions
Allergens: ACGL

Quantity of ingredients:
Noodles (whole grain) with egg 5/8 oz / 200g. (yes)
Pineapple 5/8 oz / 200g. (yes)
Water 1/2 cup / 50g. (yes)
Turkey breast meat 5/8 oz / 200g. (yes)
Rapeseed oil 1 table spoon / 12g. (little)
Garlic 1 piece / 2g. (recommended)
Basic recipe for a vegetable soup (nutritious) 1/2 cup / 100g. (recommended)
Cow's milk (whole milk 3.5% fat) 2/3 cup / 180g. (little)
Fresh cheese 0,2 lbs / 75g. (little)
Curry 3 teaspoons / 6g. (yes)
Salt 1 pinch / 1g. (little)
Pepper (ground) 1 pinch / 0,5g. (yes)
Pomegranate 1 piece / 300g. (yes)
Coconut flakes 1 table spoon / 6g. (little)

Cooking instructions:
Cook the noodles in salt water. Cut the pineapple into cubes and leave for 5 min. to simmer in water. Cut the meat sliced in strips and roast themin the oil. Add the chopped garlic and the pineapple sliced. Add about 50 ml of the ananas juice and stir in the vegetable broth. Add the milk and the fresh cheese, then stir well until the fresh cheese is completely dissolved. Now add the curry and simmer for a few minutes until a creamy consistency is reached. Season with salt and pepper. Now add the noodles in the finished sauce. Cut the pomegranate and release the seeds. Distribute as many kernels on the dressed noodles. Whoever likes it can spread coconut chips over it.

9.42 Oat flakes with aromatic spices

Stops diarrhea, promotes digestion, appetizing, harmonizes the stomach, relieves diarrhea, strengthens immune system, detoxifying and stimulating the immune system.
Cooking time approx. 25 min
Calories p. portion: 280
3 portions
Allergens: AH

Quantity of ingredients:
Oat flakes (whole grain) 1 cup / 125g. (recommended)
Walnuts 1 table spoon / 15g. (little)
Hazelnuts 1 table spoon / 15g. (little)
Water 1 1/2 cups / 240g. (yes)
Wakame 1 inch / 2g. (yes)
Apple (sweet) 1 piece / 220g. (recommended)
Cardamom 3-4 capsules / 2g. (yes)
Lemon Balm (fresh) 3-4 leaves / 3g. (yes)
Acerola fruit nectar or powder 1 teaspoon / 2g. (recommended)

Cooking instructions:
Roast oatmeal and nuts. Add hot water. Add cardamom, wakame and cook for 20 min. Add grated apple, acerola and lemon herb.

9.43 Oriental rice pan

Forcing spleen, dissolves stagnation, promotes weight loss. Good to fight immunodeficiency, loss of appetite, flatulence, high blood pressure, helps to digest fat, strengthens kidney and bladder.
Numerous vitamins, minerals and secondary plant active ingredients.
Cooking time approx. 30 min
Calories p. portion: 303
6 portions
Allergens: EL

Quantity of ingredients:
Rice (whole grain) 3/8 lbs - 6oz / 180g. (recommended)
Basic recipe for a vegetable soup (nutritious) 2 1/4 cups / 500g. (recommended)
Curry 1/2 teaspoon / 2g. (yes)
Onion (spring onion) 4 pieces / 80g. (yes)
Rapeseed oil 2 table spoons / 20g. (little)
Peppers 1/4 lbs - 4oz / 120g. (yes)
Corn 3 oz / 80g. (yes)
Shiitake, dried 1/2 oz / 80g. (recommended)
Bamboo shoots 3 oz / 80g. (yes)
Peas 3 oz / 80g. (yes)
Peaches 1/8 lbs - 2oz / 60g. (yes)
Pineapple 1/8 lbs - 2oz / 60g. (yes)
Tomato 5/8 oz / 200g. (yes)
Lovage 1 teaspoon / 2g. (yes)
Basil (fresh) 1 teaspoon / 2g. (yes)

Parsley 1 teaspoon / 2g. (recommended)
Lemon Balm (fresh) 1 teaspoon / 2g. (yes)
Pepper (ground) 1 pinch / 1g. (yes)

Cooking instructions:
Soak the mushrooms in water 20 min.
Boil the rice in the vegetable stock 15 min. and season with some curry.
Peel the onion, cut into fine cubes.
Heat the oil in a pan and sauté the onion cubes.
Wash the peppers in half, remove the core, cut into cubes and add.
Add corn, mushrooms and bamboo shoots, simmer 5 min. until firm.
Also add the bean sprouts, peas, peach cubes and pineapple cubes.
Then add the peeled, chopped tomatoes.
Add the cooked rice and season with the herbs and pepper.

9.44 Parsley cream sauce

Reduces blood pressure, strengthens immune system, forcing spleen,
dissolves stagnation, improves digestion, lowers cholesterol. Stimulates
liver function, detoxifying.
Cooking time approx. 25 min
Calories p. portion: 118
2 portions
Allergens: GL

Quantity of ingredients:
Basic recipe for a vegetable soup (nutritious) 3/4 lbs / 300g.
(recommended)
Potato 1/4 lbs - 4oz / 100g. (yes)
Parsley 1 Bunch / 15g. (recommended)
Nutmeg 1 pinch / 0,5g. (yes)
Coriander 1/2 teaspoon / 1g. (yes)
Sour cream 15% fat 1/8 lbs - 2oz / 50g. (little)
Fennel seeds ground 1/2 teaspoon / 1g. (yes)
Ginger powder 1 pinch / 0,5g. (yes)

Cooking instructions:
Broth the vegetables soup according to the basic recipe with peeled,
diced potatoes, half of the finely chopped parsley and nutmeg. Cover
and simmer until the potatoes are tender.
Using the blender, puree the vegetable broth, potatoes, remaining
freshly chopped parsley, fennel, ginger and sour cream into a smooth
sauce.

9.45 Pear compote

Promotes digestion, supports urination.
Cooking time approx. 20 min
Calories p. portion: 100
3 portions
Allergens:

Quantity of ingredients:
Water 1 1/2 cups / 240g. (yes)
Pear 4 / 500g. (recommended)

Cooking instructions:
Halve organic pears. Cores and skin can be used. Pear in the pot and add water. Simmer for up to 20 minutes until pears are tender.

9.46 Provencal noodle pan

Improves blood circulation, reduces Inflammation, relieves pain, strengthens the muscles, tendons and bones, diuretic, supports urination.
Cooking time approx. 45 min
Calories p. portion: 196
2 portions
Allergens: ACL

Quantity of ingredients:
Noodles (whole grain) with egg 5/8 oz / 200g. (yes)
Aubergine 1/8 lbs - 2oz / 60g. (yes)
Zucchini 1/8 lbs - 2oz / 60g. (yes)
Peppers 1/8 lbs - 2oz / 50g. (yes)
Beef meat 1/8 lbs - 2oz / 50g. (yes)
Garlic 2 pieces / 4g. (recommended)
Rapeseed oil 1/8 oz / 5g. (little)
Basic recipe for a vegetable soup (nutritious) 1/4 cup / 60g. (recommended)
Tomato juice 1/3 cup / 75g. (recommended)
Oregano fresh 1 pinch / 1g. (yes)
Rosemary 1 pinch / 1g. (yes)
Pepper (ground) 1 pinch / 0,5g. (yes)
Salt 1 pinch / 0,5g. (little)

Cooking instructions:
Boil noodles in plenty of salted water, chill and drain.
Wash vegetables, dice aubergine and zucchini.
Core the pepper and cut into cubes of approx. 1 cm.
Braise garlic, minced beef and prepared vegetables in heated oil, pour in vegetable stock and tomato juice and finish cooking.
Add pasta to the sauce.
Heat the whole and season with the spices and salt.

9.47 Puréed banana

Eat 2 times a day, regulates gastrointestinal function
Cooking time approx. 7 min
Calories p. portion: 144
1 portions
Allergens:

Quantity of ingredients:
Banana 1 piece / 150g. (recommended)

Cooking instructions:
Mix the banana with the fork or purée with a blender. Leave to brown for at least 5 minutes.

9.48 Quick zucchini soup

Diuretic, supports urination. Strengthens gastrointestinal function, prevents diseases (in the elderly). Stimulates liver function, detoxifying.
Cooking time approx. 10 min
Calories p. portion: 42
4 portions
Allergens:

Quantity of ingredients:
Zucchini 2-3 pieces / 500g. (yes)
Onion white 1 piece / 50g. (yes)
Corn germ oil 2 table spoons / 6g. (little)
Parsley 1 table spoon / 7g. (recommended)
Chives 1 teaspoon / 3g. (yes)
Water 2 cup / 400g. (yes)

Cooking instructions:
Fry chopped onion in oil. Add sliced zucchini and sauté well. Pour with water. Chop parsley and chives, add and puree everything.

9.49 Quinoa piquant with avocado

Anti-inflammatory, good to fight swelling, pain and itching. Reduces blood pressure, strengthens immune system. Strengthens gastrointestinal function, expands blood vessels. Good to fight gastrointestinal complaints.
Cooking time approx. 20 min
Calories p. portion: 561
2 portions
Allergens:

Quantity of ingredients:
Water 1 1/2 cups / 240g. (yes)
Quinoa 1 cup / 100g. (yes)
Carrot 1 piece shredded / 100g. (yes)
Onion (spring onion) 2 table spoons (chopped) / 12g. (yes)
Curcuma 1/2 teaspoon / 1g. (yes)
Avocado 1 piece soft / 300g. (recommended)
Salt 1 pinch / 0,5g. (little)
Pepper (ground) 1 pinch / 0,2g. (yes)
Linseed oil 2 teaspoons / 4g. (little)

Cooking instructions:
Put quinoa in hot water.
Add grated carrot, pepper and salt, finely chopped spring onion and turmeric.
Simmer about 20 minutes, pull from the fire.
Add pre-cut avocado.
Add a dash of oil and sprinkle with fresh parsley and gomasio.

Spices and herbs: turmeric, cardamom, cress, parsley, chives.
Variation: For those who want more hearty, you can also use a sardine from organic fish preserves. If you are the "protein type", this breakfast will hold on for a long time!

9.50 Red lentils with avocado and radish

Inflammations, promotes digestion, detoxifying, supports urination, reduces thirst. Strengthens heart and kidney, diuretic, calms the stomach, promotes digestion.
Cooking time approx. 20 min
Calories p. portion: 269
3 portions
Allergens: N

Quantity of ingredients:
Ginger fresh 2 slices / 2g. (yes)
Water 1 1/2 cups / 200g. (yes)
Lentils red 1 cup peeled / 100g. (yes)
Wakame 1 inch / 1g. (yes)
Salt 1 pinch / 0,5g. (little)
Lemon juice 1 dach / 1g. (yes)
Curcuma 1 pinch / 0,3g. (yes)
Avocado 1 piece / 300g. (recommended)
Pepper (ground) 1 pinch / 0,2g. (yes)
Pepper powder (hot) 1 pinch / 0,2g. (yes)
Sesame oil 1 dash / 1g. (little)
Radish (white, green, purple-red) 1 cup / 100g. (yes)

Cooking instructions:
Put in a pot with water, some chopped ginger, peeled red lentils, a piece of wakame or a small amount of hijiki and simmer until the lentils are soft. Season with salt, lemon juice and turmeric.

Meanwhile: place half an avocado per serving on one-third of the plate: add ground pepper, a pinch of salt, a little lemon juice, a pinch of sweet pepper and a little sesame oil.

Put the grated radish on the second plate third.

Fill the lentil dish into the last third of the plate.
Variant: Use radish slices instead of radishes.

9.51 Rice congee with dried fruit

Good to fight blood circulation disorders, diarrhea, antipyretic, high blood pressure, a headache, for the drainage of the body overweight and high blood pressure, stops coughing, supports urination. Provides Vitamin C.
Cooking time approx. 10 min
Calories p. portion: 210
2 portions
Allergens: GO

Quantity of ingredients:
Basic recipe for a rice soup (Congee) 4 cups / 500g. (recommended)
Butter organic 1/2 teaspoon / 5g. (little)
Apricot dried 6 table spoons / 50g. (recommended)
Water 1/2 cup / 50g. (yes)
Maple syrup 1 dash / 3g. (recommended)

Cooking instructions:
Cook rice congee according to basic recipe.

Melt a small amount of butter over a low heat and briefly fry small dried fruit with 1/2 cup of water. Add the amount of rice porridge desired for the meal and heat. Serve hot and sweeten with maple syrup if necessary.
Variant: In addition fresh fruit with braise.

9.52 Rice congee with honey pear and black sesame

Promotes digestion, supports urination, good to fight blood circulation disorders, thromboses, risk of embolism, high blood pressure, a headache, heart attack and stroke.
Cooking time approx. 10 min - 3 hours
Calories p. portion: 158
2 portions
Allergens: N

Quantity of ingredients:
Basic recipe for a rice soup (Congee) 1 1/2 cups / 240g. (recommended)
Pear 2 pieces / 300g. (recommended)
Sesame, black 1 teaspoon / 3g. (little)

Cooking instructions:
Cook rice congee according to basic recipe.
Fill pot with 3 cm of water and heat till it boils. Quarter the pears (with the skin and seeds) and simmer them covered with black sesame for 10 minutes. Mix with the rice.

9.53 Rice noodle soup with shiitake mushrooms

Very light and powerful. Strengthens the immune system.
Cooking time approx. 20 min
Calories p. portion: 66
2 portions
Allergens: L

Quantity of ingredients:
Rice noodles 2 handful / 20g. (recommended)
Shiitake, dried 4-6 pieces / 5g. (recommended)
Basic recipe for a vegetable soup (nutritious) 1 1/2 cups / 240g.
(recommended)
Chinese cabbage 1 cup / 60g. (yes)
Lovage 1 teaspoon / 3g. (yes)
Miso 2 table spoons / 18g. (yes)

Cooking instructions:
Soak rice noodles and shiitake mushrooms separately in cold water.
Heat the vegetable broth and add the soaked shiitake mushrooms cut
into strips and simmer gently. Cut Chinese cabbage into noodles, add
lovage green and rice noodles and let it steep for a while. Before
serving, stir in Miso dissolved in a little cooled water. Recommendation:
Suitable at the beginning of each meal, also for breakfast

9.54 Rice with parsnips

Rich in vitamins, minerals potassium and zinc. Good to fight blood
circulation disorders, thrombose, risk of embolism, high blood pressure,
a headache, heart attack and stroke, yeast infections.
Cooking time approx. 45 min
Calories p. portion: 206
3 portions
Allergens:

Quantity of ingredients:
Rice variety any 1 cup / 120g. (recommended)
Water 1 1/2 cups / 200g. (yes)
Salt 1 pinch / 1g. (little)
Parsnip 3-4 pieces / 450g. (recommended)
Olive oil 1 table spoon / 10g. (little)
Sage 1 teaspoon / 3g. (yes)

Cooking instructions:
Peel the parsnips and cut into slices. Fry for a short time in oil. Add the rice and fry again for a short time. Add the water and cook it at least 30 min. Sprinkle with fresh chopped sage.

9.55 Rice with stewed vegetables

Reduces blood pressure, strengthens immune system, prevents cancer, reduces radiation damage, extremely low fat content, good to fight blood circulation disorders, thrombose, risk of embolism, a headache, heart attack and stroke. Is diuretic.
Cooking time approx. 20 min
Calories p. portion: 166
2 portions
Allergens: L

Quantity of ingredients:
Rice variety any 1/2 cup / 60g. (recommended)
Water 3 cups / 300g. (yes)
Lemon peel 1 piece / 3g. (yes)
Water 1/2 cup / 0g. (yes)
Carrot 2 pieces / 180g. (yes)
Celery sticks 1/2 piece / 5g. (yes)
Champignon 1/2 cup / 50g. (yes)
Cress 2 table spoons / 20g. (recommended)
Linseed oil 1 dash / 3g. (little)

Cooking instructions:
Cook rice according to basic recipe with a piece of lemon peel.
Steam chopped carrots, celery and mushrooms until soft.
Then sprinkle with cress. Then add a dash of high quality cold oil.

9.56 Roasted millet with Celery sticks

Promotes spleen and kidney, diuretic, promoting metabolism.
Cooking time approx. 30 min
Calories p. portion: 400
2 portions
Allergens: L

Quantity of ingredients:
Millet 1 cup / 120g. (recommended)
Water 1 1/2 cups / 240g. (yes)
Celery sticks 2 rods / 50g. (yes)
Water 2 table spoons / 30g. (yes)
Herbs various 1 table spoon / 10g. (yes)
Salt 1 pinch / 1g. (little)
Sage 3-4 leaves / 2g. (yes)
Cress 1 teaspoon / 3g. (recommended)

Cooking instructions:
Roast millet briefly, pour over water, heat till it boils and let stand for 20 min. to swell.

Cut celery into small pieces and mix with water, salt and fresh herbs and cook for 10 min. Add to the millet. Sprinkle fresh sage or watercress over it.

9.57 Sliced lamb with rosemary potatoes

Improves digestion, regenerates skin, supports urination, lowers cholesterol, reduces blood pressure, strengthens immune system. Strengthens gastrointestinal function, expands blood vessels.
Cooking time approx. 1 hour
Calories p. portion: 461
4 portions
Allergens: LO

Quantity of ingredients:
Lamb meat 7/8 lbs - 1 lbs / 500g. (yes)
Olive oil 2 table spoons / 20g. (little)
Onion white 1 piece / 50g. (yes)
Garlic 1 clove / 2g. (recommended)
Nutmeg 1 pinch / 0,2g. (yes)
Carrot 3 pieces / 150g. (yes)
Celery root 1/4 tuber / 120g. (yes)
Rosemary 1 Twig / 3g. (yes)
Savory 1 teaspoon / 2g. (yes)
Parsley 1 table spoon / 8g. (recommended)
Pepper powder (hot) 1 pinch / 2g. (yes)
Red wine 1/2 cup / 125g. (little)

Salt (herbal) 1 pinch / 1g. (little)
Lemon juice 1/2 piece / 15g. (yes)
Cranberry 1 table spoon / 10g. (yes)
Potato 6 pieces / 400g. (yes)

Cooking instructions:
Cut the lamb into strips, cut the carrots and celery into small cubes.
Heat the olive oil in a pan, fry the lamb in it, add the cut onions and
garlic, salt with herbal salt, a little water, parsley, deglaze with red wine,
season with paprika and small cut rosemary, mugwort, savory, carrots
and celery, turn the heat back on small Simmer for about 35 minutes.
Season with pepper and nutmeg, if necessary still salt, add a little
lemon juice, season with paprika, cranberries.

Cut the potatoes in half, the length of, spread a little olive oil on the cut
surface, salt, sprinkle 2-3 rosemary needles on each half potato, place
the potatoes on the baking sheet and bake in a preheated oven for
approx. 25 minutes at 190°C/374°F.

9.58 Spelled with fruit and nuts

Stops diarrhea, promotes digestion, appetizing, relieves fatigue, anti-
inflammatory (gastrointestinal). Good to fight tumor lesions and
leukemia, is antiallergic in food allergies, regulates metabolism, lowers
blood glucose and cholesterol.
Cooking time approx. 1 1/2 hours
Calories p. portion: 290
3 portions
Allergens: AH

Quantity of ingredients:
Spelled grain 1 cup / 120g. (yes)
Water 1 cup / 50g. (yes)
Apple (sweet) 1 piece / 220g. (recommended)
Apricot 1 piece / 200g. (recommended)
Peaches 1 piece / 120g. (yes)
Cinnamon ground 1 pinch / 1g. (yes)
Cardamom 1 pinch / 1g. (yes)
Salt 1 pinch / 1g. (little)
Strawberries 1 cup / 120g. (recommended)
Almond puree 1 table spoon / 15g. (little)
Cocoa 1 pinch / 1g. (recommended)
Walnuts 1 table spoon / 10g. (little)

Cooking instructions:
Put spelled in hot water and cook.

Then: Give sweet chopped fruit (apples, apricots, peaches) in a little hot water, with a little cinnamon, sauté briefly; ground cardamom and / or coriander, a small pinch of salt, the boiled spelled, berries after season. Put some cocoa and roasted nuts over it.

9.59 Spicy Tofu Vegetable Pan

Forcing spleen, relieves constipation, detoxifying, reduces inflammation, improves blood circulation, promotes sweating, dissolves stagnation, reduces flatulence, reduces blood pressure, strengthens immune system, prevents cancer, reduces radiation damage.
Cooking time approx. 25 min
Calories p. portion: 241
4 portions
Allergens: EN

Quantity of ingredients:
Sesame oil 2 table spoons / 20g. (little)
Carrot 2 pieces / 100g. (yes)
Fennel 1 piece / 250g. (recommended)
Leek 1 piece / 200g. (yes)
Salt 1 pinch / 1g. (little)
Turmeric (yellow root) 1 pinch / 1g. (recommended)
Lemon juice 1 dach / 1g. (yes)
Soy Tofu 1 package / 120g. (yes)
Pepper (ground) 1 pinch / 0,5g. (yes)
Soy sauce 1 dash / 3g. (little)
Rice (whole grain) 1 cup / 120g. (recommended)
Water 6 cups / 500g. (yes)
Salt 1 pinch / 1g. (little)

Cooking instructions:
Heat sesame oil in a hot wok or a hot pan; fry the chopped carrots, fennel and leek slices; salt, a dash of lemon juice, turmeric, tofu cubes roast for 1 - 2 minutes.
Add the pepper and cook covered for about 5 minutes; drizzle with soy sauce.
Place the rice in salted water, heat till it boils and let it simmer over low heat for about 15 minutes.

9.60 Spring salad

Blood-forming, blood detoxifying, diuretic, good to fight stomach discomfort, improves digestion, diarrhea, helps to digest fat, supports urination, reduces blood pressure, detoxifying, reduces inflammation, diuretic.
Cooking time approx. 10 min
Calories p. portion: 162
4 portions
Allergens: AEMN

Quantity of ingredients:
Sorrel 3/8 lbs - 6oz / 150g. (yes)
Dandelion (young plants) 1/4 lbs - 4oz / 100g. (recommended)
Mung bean sprouting 0,2 lbs / 75g. (yes)
Cress 1/4 lbs - 4oz / 100g. (recommended)
Chives 1 Bunch / 50g. (yes)
Tomato 2 pieces / 100g. (yes)
Parsley 1 Bunch / 50g. (recommended)
Sesame paste (Tahini) 2 table spoons / 16g. (little)
Soy sauce 1 dash / 3g. (little)
Mustard 1/2 teaspoon / 2g. (yes)
White bread (wheat bread) 6 slices / 120g. (little)

Cooking instructions:
Wash all salad´s, mix and prepare the sauce as follows:
Mix tahini with mustard and balsamic vinegar, tamari, olive oil, chives and half of parsley. Pour the sauce over the salad and sprinkle the remaining parsley just before serving.
Serve with the white bread.

9.61 Tea Green tea

Green tea promotes digestion, supports urination, dissolves mucus, detoxifying, stimulates nerves, reduces blood lipids, lowers cholesterol, reduces inflammation.
Cooking time approx. 10 min
Calories p. portion: 2
1 portions
Allergens:

Quantity of ingredients:
Green tea 1 teaspoon / 2g. (recommended)
Water 1 cup / 120g. (yes)

Cooking instructions:
For each cup you use a teaspoonful or a teabag.
Pour green tea only with 60 to 80 ° C / 140 to 176 °F hot water,
otherwise it will be bitter.
If the tea has a stimulating effect, let it draw for two to three minutes. It
has a calming effect for a duration of five minutes (no longer, otherwise
it will be bitter!).
Another method: Pour the tea leaves with about 70 ° C / 158 °F hot
water and pour the water immediately again. Then just pour hot water
again. The bitter substances disappear and the tea gets a milder
aroma.

9.62 Tofu-Black Bean Chili with Rice

Supports urination, lowers cholesterol, for the drainage of the body
overweight and high blood pressure, strengthens immune system.
Cooking time approx. 45 min
Calories p. portion: 344
4 portions
Allergens: AEL

Quantity of ingredients:
Rapeseed oil 1/4 cup / 60g. (little)
Onion white 2 pieces / 120g. (yes)
Peppers 1 piece / 20g. (yes)
Pepper Cayenne 1 pinch / 0,5g. (yes)
Coriander 1 teaspoon / 2g. (yes)
Thyme 1 teaspoon / 2g. (yes)
Clove 1 teaspoon / 2g. (yes)
Spelled wholemeal flour 2 table spoons / 16g. (yes)
Sherry (whine) 1 table spoon / 8g. (little)
Soy Tofu 5/8 lbs - 8oz / 250g. (yes)
Black beans 2 cans (400g) / 400g. (recommended)
Basic recipe for a chicken soup (warming) 1 1/2 cups / 300g.
(recommended)
Bay leaf 1 piece / 0,2g. (yes)
Garlic 6 pieces / 8g. (recommended)
Water 6 cups / 400g. (yes)
Rice Basmati 1 cup / 120g. (recommended)

Cooking instructions:

Heat the oil at medium temperature in a large saucepan, add onions, paprika and chilli powder and fry for 2 minutes until the onions are glassy.

Add the remaining spices, stirring constantly, stirring until the aroma rises.

Dust the flour, fry for 2 minutes and make sure that the paste-like spice mixture does not burn.

Deglaze with sherry, add the black beans (tin) and mix with the spices.

Add the chicken broth, add the bay leaf and stir in the chopped garlic.

Simmer the beans for 30 minutes and add some chicken stock if needed.

Cook the tofu cubes during the last 10 minutes. The tofu can easily disintegrate and should therefore be lifted very gently with a wooden spoon.

Finally, pick out the bay leaf and serve the tofu black bean chili with rice.

9.63 Turkey breast with vegetables (Asian)

Strengthens blood, strengthens bone marrow, dissolves stagnation, promotes digestion and is goo to fight high blood pressure. Rice to drain the body at overweight and high blood pressure.

Cooking time approx. 45 min
Calories p. portion: 535
2 portions
Allergens: AEN

Quantity of ingredients:

Rice variety any 1 cup / 120g. (recommended)
Water 6 cups / 240g. (yes)
Turkey breast meat 5/8 oz / 200g. (yes)
Ginger fresh 1/3 inch / 3g. (yes)
Garlic 1 piece / 2g. (recommended)
Soy sauce 2 table spoons / 20g. (little)
Wheat flour 2 teaspoons / 15g. (yes)
Onion (spring onion) 2 pieces / 40g. (yes)
Peppers 1/2 piece / 10g. (yes)
Champignon 8 pieces / 30g. (yes)
Sesame oil 2 table spoons / 20g. (little)

Soy sauce 1 table spoon / 12g. (little)
Curry 1 pinch / 2g. (yes)
Turmeric (yellow root) 1 pinch / 2g. (recommended)
Cashews 2 teaspoons / 25g. (yes)

Cooking instructions:
Cook the rice in salted water.
Cut the turkey meat into thin strips. Peel and dice the ginger and garlic.
Put together with the meat strips in a bowl. Mix 1 tbsp of soy sauce with
the wheat starch and stir until smooth. Add to the meat and marinate for
30 minutes. Wash spring onions and peppers, clean and cut into small
pieces. Clean and quarter the mushrooms.
Put one tablespoon of sesame oil in a pan and sauté and warm the
marinated turkey. Now add the remaining oil to the pan and fry the other
vegetables in it. Now add the meat and season with soy sauce and
spices. Serve with the rice. Sprinkle the cashews over the dish before
serving.

9.64 Vegetable bowl with tofu and curry on rice

Diuretic, reduces blood glucose. Reduces flatulence, supports
digestion. Contains ideal herbal mucus, which provides regeneration of
the small and large intestinal flora. Reduces blood pressure,
strengthens immune system.
Cooking time approx. 30 min
Calories p. portion: 162
6 portions
Allergens: E

Quantity of ingredients:
Olive oil 2 table spoons / 20g. (little)
Garlic 2 cloves / 3g. (recommended)
Onion white 1 piece / 60g. (yes)
Curry 2 table spoons / 16g. (yes)
Water 2 cup / 500g. (yes)
Turnips 2 pieces / 50g. (yes)
Pumpkin 1 piece / 400g. (yes)
Carrot 1 piece / 100g. (yes)
Parsnip 1 piece / 150g. (recommended)
Potato 1 piece / 70g. (yes)
Sweet potato 1 piece / 70g. (yes)

Cauliflower 1/4 piece / 250g. (recommended)
Broccoli 1/2 piece / 250g. (yes)
Okra 12 pieces / 200g. (yes)
Soy Tofu 1 piece / 250g. (yes)
Basil 2 table spoons / 12g. (yes)
Salt 1 pinch / 0,5g. (little)

Cooking instructions:
Heat the oil at medium temperature in a large, heavy casserole, add the garlic and onion and sauté with constant stirring. Sprinkle curry powder over it, fry gently for about 5 minutes and make sure that the garlic and curry do not burn. Add the water and heat till it boils. Gradually peel all vegetables, dice and add, starting with the varieties that need the longest cooking time. Once the water has boiled again, reduce the heat and simmer the vegetables for about 15 minutes. When it is almost soft. Add the cauliflower and broccoli florets and the okra and cook the stew for another 10 to 15 minutes. Add the tofu during the last 5 minutes.

Cook the brown rice at the same time: Sprinkle the rice in a medium saucepan with water, salt and cover for about 20 minutes. cook on a low heat. Take from the fire and another 10 min. to let go.

Arrange the stew over the brown rice and sprinkle with basil.

9.65 Vegetable juice

Promotes digestion, helps to digest fat, supports urination, reduces blood pressure, strengthens immune system, prevents cancer, reduces radiation damage, forcing spleen, is stimulating.
Cooking time approx. 15 min
Calories p. portion: 64
1 portions
Allergens: L

Quantity of ingredients:
Celery root 1/2 oz / 20g. (yes)
Carrot 1/4 lbs - 4oz / 100g. (yes)
Tomato 1/4 lbs - 4oz / 100g. (yes)
Garlic 1 piece / 2g. (recommended)
Salt 1 teaspoon / 2g. (little)
Acerola fruit nectar or powder 1/2 teaspoon / 1g. (recommended)

Cooking instructions:
Peel all ingredients and use the juicer to make a drink. Stir in the acerola.

9.66 Vegetable rice

Forcing spleen, dissolves stagnation, promotes weight loss. Good to fight immunodeficiency, loss of appetite, flatulence, high blood pressure, strengthens kidney and bladder. Diuretic, warming the body from the inside, regulates internal organs functions.
Cooking time approx. 30 min
Calories p. portion: 304
3 portions
Allergens: L

Quantity of ingredients:
Broccoli 1/8 lbs - 2oz / 50g. (yes)
Carrot 1/8 lbs - 2oz / 50g. (yes)
Kohlrabi 1/8 lbs - 2oz / 50g. (recommended)
Cauliflower 1 oz / 30g. (recommended)
Peas 1/2 oz / 20g. (yes)
Margarine 1 teaspoon / 4g. (little)
Rice (whole grain) 5/8 oz / 200g. (recommended)
Basic recipe for a vegetable soup (nutritious) 7/8 lbs / 400g. (recommended)
Parsley 1/2 oz / 20g. (recommended)
Pepper (ground) 1 pinch / 0,2g. (yes)

Cooking instructions:
Cut the broccoli, carrots and kohlrabi into small cubes, divide the cauliflower into small florets. Heat the margarine in a pan or saucepan, sauté the vegetables. Then add the rice, top up with the vegetable stock and leave to soak for 15-20 minutes.

In the meantime finely chop the parsley. After cooking, season the rice with freshly ground pepper and parsley.

9.67 Vegetarian vegetable-oatmeal-potatoes mash

Improves digestion, regenerates skin, supports urination, lowers cholesterol, supports urination, relieves constipation, strengthens mother milk production.
Cooking time approx. 25 min
Calories p. portion: 91
2 portions
Allergens: A

Quantity of ingredients:
Carrot (Early Carrot) 1 oz / 30g. (yes)
Parsnip 1 oz / 30g. (recommended)
Zucchini 1 oz / 30g. (yes)
Fennel 1/2 oz / 10g. (recommended)
Potato 1/8 lbs - 2oz / 50g. (yes)
Water 1/2 oz / 20g. (yes)
Oat flakes (whole grain) 1/2 oz / 10g. (recommended)
Orange juice 1 oz / 30g. (recommended)
Rapeseed oil 1/4 oz / 8g. (little)

Cooking instructions:
Wash the vegetables and potatoes, dice and fry in a little water. Add water and oatmeal, puree everything and finally add the oil. Note: This porridge replaces the vegetable-potato-meat porridge when meat is to be dispensed with in the infant's diet. Since meat is the best food source for iron, a vegetarian diet must pay particular attention to a sufficient supply of iron.

9.68 Vitamin drink

Regulates gastrointestinal function, promotes spleen and liver, reduces blood pressure, strengthens immune system, prevents cancer, reduces radiation damage, supports urination, quenches thirst, calms the stomach, prevents cancer.
Cooking time approx. 5 min
Calories p. portion: 172
3 portions
Allergens:
Quantity of ingredients:
Orange juice 1 cup / 300g. (recommended)
Carrot 5/8 oz / 200g. (yes)
Banana 2 pieces / 300g. (recommended)
Kiwi 1 piece / 20g. (recommended)

Cooking instructions:
Chop oranges, carrots, bananas and kiwi and finely puree with the blender.

9.69 Warming porridge

Strengthens immune system. Diuretic and laxative. Provides vitamin C. Dissolves stones. Promotes digestion, detoxifying, promotes perspiration, reduces blood lipids, stimulates, dissolves stagnation.
Cooking time approx. 10 min
Calories p. portion: 357
1 portions
Allergens: AHO

Quantity of ingredients:
Oat flakes (whole grain) 6 table spoons / 60g. (recommended)
Fig dried 3 pieces / 15g. (recommended)
Star anise 1 piece / 1g. (yes)
Ginger fresh 1 pinch / 0,5g. (yes)
Water 1 cup / 120g. (yes)
Maple syrup 1 table spoon / 10g. (recommended)
Walnuts 1 table spoon (chopped) / 8g. (little)

Cooking instructions:
Soak the dried fruit. Roast Oatmeal dry. Add dried ginger, star anise or cinnamon, a little grated ginger and boil everything with water to a mash. With maple syrup sweet. Whip grated walnuts and sprinkle before serving.

Effect: Suitable for the cold season.
Caution: Fresh ginger does not drink over a long period of time.

9.70 Yellow lentil soup

Strengthens heart and kidney, diuretic, promotes spleen, calms the stomach, promotes digestion, strengthens immune system, prevents cancer, reduces radiation damage, stimulates liver function, antioxidativ.
Cooking time approx. 20 min
Calories p. portion: 155
7 portions
Allergens: A

Quantity of ingredients:
Lentils yellow 1 lbs / 500g. (yes)
Carrot 2 pieces / 150g. (yes)
Kohlrabi 1 piece / 300g. (recommended)
Onion white 1 piece / 50g. (yes)
Parsley 1/2 bunch / 100g. (recommended)
Turmeric (yellow root) 1 pinch / 1g. (recommended)
Cardamom 1 pinch / 1g. (yes)
Salt 1 pinch / 1g. (little)
Olive oil 1 table spoon / 10g. (little)
Water 4 cup / 1000g. (yes)
Lemon juice 1/2 piece / 15g. (yes)
White bread (wheat bread) 7 slices / 140g. (little)

Cooking instructions:
Wash lenses well in a colander. Heat oil in a pot. Add finely chopped onion, sliced carrots, diced kohlrabi and spices, sauté and salt. Add the lentils and cover with water and simmer for 20 minutes. Add water as needed and season with salt. Sprinkle with fresh parsley or fresh green cilantro and drizzle with lemon juice.
Here you can also use red lenses. (same cooking time).
Serve with white bread.

10 Effects of food

10.1 Use ingredients: recommendable

Acai powder
Acerola fruit nectar or powder
Aloe juice
Apple (sour)
Apple (sweet)
Apple juice (natural cloudy)
Apple puree
Apricot
Apricot dried

Apricot nectar
Apricots juice
Avocado
Banana
Banana (cooking banana)
Barley not peeled
Basic recipe for a chicken soup
(warming)
Basic recipe for a duck soup
Basic recipe for a rice soup (Congee)
Basic recipe for a vegetable soup
(nutritious)
Berries of the season
Berry juice
Bitter Herb liqueur
Black beans
Black fungus mushroom
Black-eyed peas
Blueberry juice
Borage
Broad beans (thick beans)
Butter beans white
Cauliflower
Chanterelle
Cherry juice
Chervil dried
Chocolate (Diabetic)
Cocoa
Compote (fruits of the season)
Cranberries
Cream 10% coffee cream
Cress
Currant jam (black)
Currant juice (black)
Currants (black)
Currants (red)
Dandelion (young plants)
Dates dried
Dates red

Dill
Fennel
Fig dried
Fish pieces mixed (fresh water)
Fox nut, gorgon nut, makhana
Fruit mix juice
Garlic
Ginkgo fruit
Grape juice red
Grape juice white
Green spelt
Green tea
Hibiscus
Kiwi
Kohlrabi
Kudzu
Leaf salads (bitter)
Lemon Balm (dried)
Lily bulbs
Linseed (crushed)
Mango juice
Manioc flour
Maple syrup
Mediterranean fish (cod, plaice,
haddock, sea eel, mackerel)
Millet
Millet flakes
Nettles
Oat flakes (whole grain)
Oat flakes roasted
Oat flour
Oat meal
Orange juice
Papaya
Parsley
Parsnip
Pear
Pear juice
Pearl barley
Pearl barley
Plum dried
Raisins
Reishi mushroom
Rice (whole grain)
Rice Basmati
Rice black
Rice long grain rice
Rice mash
Rice noodles

Rice round grain
Rice variety any
Rose hip
Rose hip tea
Rusk
Rye
Rye flour
Rye wholemeal bread
Sago (cereals)
Sea buckthorn
Shiitake, dried
Soy flour
Soy noodles
Soya Cuisine (soy cream)
Soybeans

Soybeans, yellow
Strawberries
Strawberry Juice
Tomato dried
Tomato juice
Tomato paste
Tomato puree
Topinambur
Turmeric (yellow root)
Vegetable juice
Wheat bran
Wheat flour whole grain
Wheat/Rye/Gray-black bread with yeast
Whole grain bread
Wholemeal flour

10.2 Use ingredients: yes

Adzuki beans
Agar agar (kelp)
Agave nectar
Agrimony
Almond marzipan
Amaranth
Amaranth Pops
Angelica root
Anise (Common Fennel)
Apricot jam
Apricots
Arrowroot
Artichoke
Asparagus (green or white)
Aubergine
Baking powder
Balm
Bamboo shoots
Banchatee (green tea)
barberry
Barley
Barley flour
Barley grass powder
Barley grouts
Barley malt
Basic recipe for a beef soup
Basic recipe for a beef soup (warming)
Basic recipe for a fish soup
Basil
Basil (fresh)
Batavia
Bay leaf
Beans (green, fresh)
Bearberry leaf
Beef fillet
Beef meat

Beef meat (calf)
Beer (alcohol-free)
Beer (alcohol-reduced)
Bitter Lemon
Bitter orange peel
Black caraway
Black tea
Blackberry dried (unripe fruit)
Blackberry jam
Blackberry leaves
Blackberry´s
Blackthorn (Sloe)
Blue mallow tee
Blueberry
Blueberry dried
Blueberry jam
Bocksdorn fruits (Fructus Lycii, Goji, goji berry dried
Boletus mushroom
Boxhorn clover seeds
Bread roll
Bread with carob kernel flour
Breadcrumbs (wheat bread, bread roll)
Broccoli
Brussels sprouts
Buckbean
Buckwheat
Buckwheat (roasted) Kasha
Buckwheat whole grain
Bulgur (cereals)
Burdock root tea
Bush beans
Calamari
Cantaloupe
Capers in olive oil
Carambola (Star fruit)

Cardamom
Carob flour, St. john's bread
Carp
Carrot
Carrot (Early Carrot)
Carrot juice without sugar
Cashews
Caviar
Celery root
Celery sticks
Cereal coffee
Chamomile
Chamomile tea
Champignon
Channa-Dal
Chard
Chenpi (chinese tangerine bowl)
Cherry
Cherry (sour)
Cherry compote
Chervil
Chestnut puree
Chestnuts
Chicken meat
Chickpeas
Chickweed
Chicory
Chili (pod or ground)
Chinese cabbage
Chinese pearl barley
Chives
Chlorella (fresh water)
Chrysanthemum blossom tea
Cinnamon ground
Cinnamon sticks
Clementine
Clementines
Clove
Coconut milk
Cod
Codfish
Coffee
Coix (seeds) YiYi Ren
Cola drink
Coriander
Coriander (fresh)
Corn
Corn (fast polenta)
Corn (roasted)
Corn flour
Corn Grease (Polenta)
Corn silk tea
Corn starch
Couscous

Crab
Cranberry
Cranberry
Cranberry jam
Cranberry juice
Creamer
Crispbread
Crucian
Cucumber
Cucumber (bitter)
Cucumber (spicy cucumber)
Cumin (Caraway seed)
Curcuma
Currant (black)
Currant (red)
Currant (white)
Currant jam (red)
Curry
Curry paste red
Daisy
Dandelion juice
Dandelionroots tea
Dashi
Deer meat
Deer meat
Deer's Bones
Deer's kidneys
Duck (heart)
Ducks egg
Dulse (seaweed)
Dyer's broom herb
Elderberries
Elderberry blossom tee
Endive salad
Fennel seeds ground
Fennel tea
Fenugreek (Trigonella foenum-graecum)
Fig
Fish innards
Fish remains
Fish sauce
Flounder
Flower pollen
French beans
Fresh cheese from soya
Freshwater crab
Freshwater fish
Fructose (glucose)
Fruit tea
Gail plum
Galangal
Garam Masala powder
Gelatin white

Gelee Royal
Gentian root
Gentian root tea
Ginger fresh
Ginger powder
Ginseng
Ginseng root
Goat
Goose
Goose blood
Goose egg
Goose parts
Gooseberry
Gourd
Grapefruit (Pomelo)
Grapefruit dried peel
Grapefruit juice
Grapes red
Grapes white
Grass carp
Greengage
Ground
Ground caraway
Guava
Halibut (Flatfish)
Hawthorn
Herbal tea mix
Herbs bitter
Herbs of Provence
Herbs various
Herbs wild
Hibiscus tea
Hijiki
Hokkaido pumpkin
Honey
Hop
Horehound leaves
Horse meat
Hyssop
Iceberg lettuce
Jasmine blossoms tee
Jellyfish
Juniper berry
Kaki plum
Kalmus
Kidney beans (red)
King Solomon's-seal
Kombu seaweed (Saccharina japonica)
Kukicha tea
Kumquats
Ladyfingers
Lamb meat
Lamb shoulder
Lamb's lettuce

Lamb's lettuce
Lavender blossoms
Leek
Lemon
Lemon Balm (fresh)
Lemon juice
Lemon peel
Lemongrass
Lentils
Lentils black
Lentils red
Lentils yellow
Lettuce
Licorice root tea
Lima beans
Lime
Lime blossom tea
Linseed
Liver smoothing tea
Longane
Loquate / Japanese medlar
Lotus roots
Lotus seeds
Lovage
Lovage seeds
Luo Han Guo fruit
Lychee
Lychee in Preserved
Lye roll
Mackerel
Mallow (Malva sylvestris) blossom tea
Malt
Mango
Marjoram
Medlar
Mineral water
Mirabelle plum
Miso
Miso black (fermented)
Miso paste (soy bean paste)
Mixed Pickles
Morel (black, dried)
Morel, dried
Mu Erh Mushroom
Muesli
Mulberry fruit
Mulled Wine Spice
Mullet
Multi-grain bread (gray bread)
Mung bean
Mung bean sprouting
Mussels
Mustard
Mustard Dijon

Mustard medium hot
Mustard seeds
Mustard sweet
Mutton
Mutton
Nasturtium (nose-twister or nose-tweaker)
Nectarine
Noodles (wheat) with egg
Noodles (wheat, lasagne) with egg
Noodles (wheat, ribbon noodles) with egg
Noodles (wheat, spaghetti) with egg
Noodles (whole grain) with egg
Nori, purple seaweed, red algae
Nutmeg
Oat
Oat fusion (baby food)
Oat milk
Octopus
Octopus
Okra
Onion (shallot)
Onion (spring onion)
Onion read
Onion white
Orange
Orange blossom
Orange dried peel
Orange grated peel
Orange jam
Orange peel
Oregano dried
Oregano fresh
Oyster mushroom
Oyster shell powder
Oysters
Parsley root
Passion blossoms tea
Passion fruit
Peaches
Peaches (canned)
Peanut butter
Peas
Peas, green
Pepper (ground)
Pepper Cayenne
Pepper powder (hot)
Pepper white (ground)
Peppercorns
Peppermint
Peppermint tea
Pepperoni
Pepperoni, red, pitted, halved

Pepperoni, yellow, pitted, halved
Peppers
Peppers (rose peppers)
Peppers (sweet)
Peppers powder
Perch
Pheasant
Pickle
Pigeon
Pigeon egg
Pimento
Pineapple
Pineapple juice without sugar
Pinto beans speckled
Plaice
Plum
Plums
Pomegranate
Poppy
Potato
Potato (mealy)
Potato flour
Prickly pear
Psyllium seed
Pudding powder vanilla
Pumpernickel (dark bread)
Pumpkin
Quince
Quinoa
Rabbit
Rabbit (wild)
Rabbit meat
Radicchio
Radish
Radish (white, green, purple-red)
Radish black
Radish horseradish
Radish leaves
Raspberry
Raspberry dried (immature)
Raspberry jam
Raspberry leaf tea
Red beet
Red berry (without sugar)
Red cabbage
Rhubarb
Ribworttea
Rice (fragrance)
Rice (Gaoliang / Sorghum)
Rice flour
Rice malt
Rice red
Rice starch
Rice sticky

Rice sweet
Rice wild (nature rice)
Romaine lettuce / lettuce salad
Rose blossom tea
Rose leaf tea
Rosefish
Rosemary
Rucola
Safflower (Dyer's thistle / Hong Hua)
Saffron
Sage
Sake
Salmon
Salsify
Sauerkraut (cutted cabbage fermented)
Savory
Savoy cabbage / kale
Sea cucumber
Seacrab
Shark
Shrimp
Shrimps
Skim milk powder
Slug
Sorrel
Sour cherries
Sourdough
Soy Tofu
Soy Tofu smoked
Soybean milk
Soybeans, black
Soybeans, blacks, fermented
Spelled (Dark) bread
Spelled flakes
Spelled grain
Spelled semolina
Spelled wholemeal flour
Spinach
Spiny lobsters
Spurdog (spiny dogfish, Schillerlocken)
St. Benedict's thistle, blessed thistle,
holy thistle, spotted thistle
Star anise
Stevia (candyleaf, sweetleaf)
Strawberry jam
Sugar fructose - fruit sugar
Sugar glucose - grapes sugar
Sugar Milk Sugar
Sugar substitute (sweetener)
Supplementary nutrition
Sweet potato
Tabasco
Tangerine
Tarragon (Estragon)

Tea mixture uric acid lowering
Thyme
Thyme dried
Toast bread (whole grain)
Tomato
Tonic Water
Trout
Trout (smoked)
Truffle
Tsampa (roasted barley flour)
Tuna
Turkey breast meat
Turkey ham
Turnip
Turnips
Umeboshi paste
Umeboshi plums (Japanese apricots)
Valerian
Vanilla
Vanilla pod
Vanilla powder
Vanilla sugar natural
Vinegar (Apple vinegar)
Vinegar (Red wine vinegar)
Vinegar Aceto Balsamico
Vinegar Aceto Balsamico white
Wakame
Water
Water hot
Watermelon
Wax gourd
Wheat
Wheat bulgur
Wheat flakes
Wheat flour
Wheat semolina
Wheat semolina for children
Wheatgrass juice
Wheatgrass powder
White beans
White cabbage
Whitefish
Wild boar meat
Wild garlic (garlic spinach)
Wild herbs
Wild strawberries
Wormwood herb
Yam root, yam root tuber
Yarrow
Yarrow tea
Yeast
Yew nut
Yogi tea
Zucchini

10.3 Use ingredients: little

Almond
Almond milk
Almond puree
Bean oil
Beef heart
Beef heart (calf)
Beef kidney
Beef liver
Beef lungs (calf)
Beef meatbones
Beef Oxtail pieces
Beef soup meat
Beef stomach
Beer (Pils)
Beer (Top-fermented German dark beer)
Bitter liqueur
Borage oil
Brazil nuts
Brie cheese
Brown ale
Butter (half fat)
Butter organic
Buttermilk
Camembert
Campari
Chicken Blood
Chicken egg
Chicken egg white
Chicken heart
Chicken liver
Chicken stomach
Chicken yolk
Chocolate
Coconut fat
Coconut flakes
Coconut grated
Coconut meat
Cola drink (low calorie)
Corn germ oil
Cottage cheese
Cow's milk (1.5% fat)
Cow's milk (whole milk 3.5% fat)
Cream (30% fat)
Cream sour 10%
Cream sour 20%
Cream sour 30%
Créme fraiche cheese
Curd cheese 20%
Curd cheese 40%

Duck (slaughtered)
Edam cheese
Eel
Emmental cheese
Evening primrose oil
Fernet Branca (herbal bitter liqueur)
Fresh cheese
Fresh cheese with herbs
Ginger oil
Ginseng liqueur
Goat and sheep's blood
Goat and sheep's brain
Goat and sheep's liver
Goat and sheep's milk
Goat and sheep's stomach
Goat cheese
Gouda cheese
Grapeseed oil
Hazelnuts
Herring
Honey wine (Met)
Kefir
Lamb bones
Lamb kidneys
Lamb liver
Linseed oil
Lobster
Lychee liqueur
Mare's milk
Margarine
Margarine (diet)
Martini
Mascarpone cheese
Mayonnaise 50%
Mozzarella
Olive oil
Olives
Olives green
Palm oil
Parmesan
Peanut oil
Peanuts
Pig blood
Pine nuts
Pineapple (from a can)
Pistachios
Pork brain
Pork heart
Pork kidneys
Pork knuckle

Pork liver
Pork lung
Pork marrow bones
Pork meat
Pork sausage (Bratwurst) Pork skin
Pork stomach
Pork/beef sausage (smoked)
Pork's intestine
Processed cheese 12%
Prosecco
Puff pastry
Pumpkin seed oil
Pumpkin seeds
Quail
Quail egg
Rabbit liver
Rapeseed oil
Red wine
Rum
Salt
Salt (herbal)
Sesame oil
Sesame oil roasted
Sesame paste (Tahini)
Sesame, black
Sesame, white
Sheep's milk
Sheep's milk yoghurt
Sherry (whine)
Sour cream 15% fat
Sour milk
Sour milk cheese 20%

Soy sauce
Soybean oil
Spirit
Sugar - icing sugar
Sugar brown
Sugar candy white
Sugar cane sugar
Sugar molasses
Sugar palm sugar
Sugar white
Sunflower oil
Sunflower seeds
Thistle oil
Walnut oil
Walnuts
Walnuts roasted
Wheat beer
Wheat flatbread/pita bread
Wheat germ oil
Whey
White bread (baguette)
White bread (pretzel sticks)
White bread (roll)
White bread (wheat bread)
White breadcrumbs
White dumpling bread (wheat bread cut into chunks)
White wine
Wormwood
Yoghurt vanilla
Yogurt (natural, 1.5% fat)
Yogurt (natural, 3.5% fat)

10.4 Do not use contra-acting foods

Anchovy / Sardine
Beef bone marrow
Clarified butter
Cooking oil
Cream, sweet 30%
Eel smoked
Feta cheese
Feta cheese
Goose fat
Gorgonzola

Mayonnaise 80%
Mold cheese
Peanut (roasted)
Pork Bacon
Pork fat (lard)
Pork ham
Pork ham cooked
Pork ham smoked
Pork Lard
Processed cheese 30%

11 Herbs and their effects

11.1 Basil

It has a beneficial effect on flatulence and nausea, relaxing and soothing.

Good to fight emphysema, bronchitis, whooping cough, high blood pressure, headache, mouth odor, warts, hiccup, gout, migraine.

11.2 Mugwort

Reduces bleeding, alleviates pain. In the kitchen, mugwort is used as a spice for fat food. Since it contains many bitter substances, it boosts fat burning and promotes digestion.

11.3 Savory

Stomach-strengthening, soothing and appetizing. Ideal for prevent colds, strengthens the immune system. In case of incontinence or nocturnal wetting (not for children), put the beans in liquor for libido.

11.4 Nettles

Promotes urination. Tea or juice, cleanses the blood and the kidneys, supports prostate problems, inhibit the formation of inflammation, pain-relieving.

11.5 Dill

The medicinal and spice herb has an antispasmodic effect and stimulates gastric juice production. Good to fight flatulence. Antispasmodic for gastrointestinal discomfort.

11.6 Chervil dried

Forces urination, detoxifying, blood-purifying and blood-pressure-reducing effects.

11.7 Coriander

The essential oils are appetizing, digestive, cramping and soothing in stomach and intestinal disorders.

11.8 Herbs various

Appetizing, lots of trace elements and vitamins

11.9 Cress

Diuretic, supports urination. Good to fight dry mouth, inner agitation, sore throat, diabetes, kidney stones, gastrointestinal complaints, lung problems, menstrual cramps or cancer.

11.10   Chives

Bactericide, prevents cancer, strengthens gastric juice production, promotes digestion and blood circulation, promotes growth, triggers stagnation.

11.11   Lovage

Stimulates digestion, reduces pain. Extracts of the root are used to flush out urinary tract infections and prevent kidney gravel.

11.12   Dandelion (young plants)

Detoxifies, relieves inflammation. Regulates digestion, helps with rheumatism, releases kidney stones, leaves pimples and chronic skin disorders disappear.

11.13   Oregano fresh

It has an anti-digestive, calming and nerve-strengthening effect, helps to fight cramping stomach and intestinal disorders. The ingredient Carvacrol has an anti-inflammatory effect.

11.14   Parsley

Stimulates liver function, detoxifies. Forces urinating. Relieves flatulence. Digestive and menstrual stimulating, birth-accelerating, memory-enhancing, blood-purifying, skin-smoothing.

11.15   Peppermint

Relaxes, frees the lungs and the nose (inhale), regulates the cycle. Stimulates bile flow and bile production, antispasmodic in gastrointestinal disorders, antimicrobial and antiviral.

11.16   Rosemary

Promotes digestion, relieves bloating, strengthens lung, spleen and kidney. Affects the circulation and nerves. Appetizing. Baths help to fight circulatory disorders as well as with gout and rheumatism.

11.17 Sage

Good to fight yeast infections. The leaves have a digestive effect and are used in greasy foods. Antiperspirant effect. Helps to relieve coughing attacks. Dries out (TCM).

11.18 Sorrel

Astringent, hematopoietic, purifies the blood, diuretic. Good to fight liver weakness, upset stomach, indigestion, constipation, diarrhea, worms, scurvy, anemia, women's complaints, wounds, skin rashes, boils, ulcers, swelling.

11.19 Black caraway

Detoxifying, immunoregulatory. In addition, the oil should stimulate the formation of bone marrow cells and generally protect body cells from viruses.

11.20 Thyme dried

Disinfecting. It stimulates the blood circulation, increases the appetite and helps to digest fat meat better. Strengthens lungs and spleen (TCM).

11.21 Lemon Balm (fresh)

Stimulating, antibacterial, encouraging, relaxing, antispasmodic, cooling, antipyretic, analgesic, sweat-inducing, virus-inhibiting. Good for colds, fever, flu, cough, bronchitis, asthma, loss of appetite, bloating, heartburn.

12 Basics of Nutrition

The basic principles of nutrition described herein are general recommendations. They are not aimed at a specific form of therapy. Recommendations concerning a therapy have priority.

12.1 Nutrition

Regular meals in a relaxed atmosphere. A warm breakfast is considered a good start into the day.

The main meals ought to be taken for lunch – supper in the early evening. Pay attention to feeling hungry or sated: don't eat too much nor remain hungry is the rule

Prepare the meals freshly from natural, regional products. Frozen, heat-conserved, industrially prepared or foodstuffs cooked in the microwave oven are rejected.

Choice of foodstuffs according to the season: more cooling food in summer, more warming food in winter.

Eat cooked food at least twice a day. Food and drinks ought to be lukewarm, never ice-cold or hot.

Raw vegetables, briefly cooked vegetables, freshly squeezed juices and mineral water are not recommended. Milk and dairy products are only included in the diet if they don't cause problems.

Don't use therapeutic recipes over a longer period without consulting your doctor or therapist.

Varied food

Enjoy the diversity of foodstuffs. Characteristics of a balanced nutrition are variety, suitable combination and a balancedQuantity of rich and low energy foodstuffs (on one hand avoiding undersupply with essential nutrients and on the other hand to take to many undesirable substances).

A lot of Cereal Products - and Potatoes

Bread, pasta, rice, cereal flakes (best wholemeal) as well as potatoes contain almost no fat, but many vitamins, mineral nutrients, trace elements, roughage and secondary plant substances. These foodstuffs ought to be taken with low-fat side dishes.

Vegetables and Fruit – „Take Five" every day …

5 portions of vegetables and fruit a day, as fresh as possible, briefly cooked, or maybe one portion as a juice – ideal as a side dish to every meal as well as snack between meals: Thus a lot of vitamins, mineral nutrients as well as roughage and secondary plant substances

Daily milk and dairy products

Milk and Dairy Products every Day, once or twice per Week Fish; meat, sausages as well as eggs moderately. These foodstuffs contain valuable nutrients like calcium in the milk, iodine selenium and omega-3 fat acids in saltwater fish. Meat is favorable due to its high content of disposable iron and the vitamins B1, B6 and B12. Quantities of 300 – 600 g meat and sausage per week are sufficient. Prefer low-fat products, especially in meat- and dairy products.

Low-fat and fatty Foodstuffs

Fat supplies us with essential fat acids and fatty foodstuffs contain also fat-soluble vitamins. Fat is high in energy; therefore much fat in the food may cause overweight, possibly also cancer. Too many saturated fat acids may further a tendency for cardio-vascular diseases in the long term. Prefer vegetable oils and fats (e.g. rapeseed-, olive-, soya-oils and solid fats produced therefrom). Beware of invisible fat in meat- and dairy products, pastry and sweets as well as in fast-food and convenience foods. 70 – 90 g fat per day is sufficient.

Moderately Sugar and Salt

Take sugar and foods/drinks containing various kinds of sugar (e.g. glucose syrup) only occasionally. Use herbs and spices as well as a little salt creatively. Prefer salt containing iodine.

Plenty of Liquids

Water is absolutely essential. Drink 1-2 l liquids every day. Prefer water (with or without gas) and other low-calorie drinks. Alcoholic drinks should not be taken.

Tasty Dishes, carefully cooked

Cook the meals with as low temperatures and as short as possible, using little water and fat – this preserves the original taste, keeps the nutrients intact and prevents the production of harmful compounds.

Take time and enjoy the food

Take your Time and enjoy your Food
Eating consciously helps to eat right. The eye enjoys food, too. It's fun, invites to enjoy varied dishes and stimulates the feeling of satiety.

Watch your Weight and stay in Motion

A balanced diet and a lot of exercise and sport (30 – 60 min/day) are a healthy combination. The right weight furthers well-being and health. Thermals, directional effectiveness, digestive power

There are various criteria for judging the effectiveness of herbs and foodstuffs.

The use of certain herbs and ingredients is based on observations of the effects on the body which these foodstuffs, herbs and spices show after having eaten them. The medical science has developed following system: Every ingredient or herb has a directional effectiveness. Furthermore, there are herbs which have a special effect on certain organs.

The basic condition for a healthy metabolism is to obtain sufficient energy from food and that the digestive process doesn't use too much energy. An easily digestible meal makes content and sated, doesn't cause flatulence and fatigue after the meal. The perfect spices increase the healthiness of our meals. Very often, just small doses of herbs and spices will suffice. They are not used to make us sated, but to help our digestive organs to digest the food.

12.2 Recipes

The recipes list the ingredients to be used and the cooking instructions show how the dish is prepared. The list of ingredients shows the concerned quantities as well as the relevance for the therapy. If you find „less than mentioned", try to comply or find an alternative from the „list of recommended foodstuffs". Mostly it shall result just in a small change of taste when you simply avoid this ingredient.

Mild cooking methods: boiling, stewing, poaching, steaming
Strong cooking methods: barbecuing, roasting, frying, smoking
Balanced cooking methods: deep-frying, baking brick
Deep-freezing and warming in the microwave oven should be avoided (denaturalization).

12.3 Foodstuffs

Foodstuffs have an effect on body and soul like medicinal herbs, only a very much milder one. Dietary advice is mainly based on regional foodstuffs. The knowledge about the effects of each foodstuff and the knowledge, when which foodstuff shall be used, is based on the orthodoschool of medicine. Use ecologic-organic products, if possible. As everything should be cooked for a long time due to a better digestability and very rarely eaten raw, the food agrees with everyone.

The classification of the foodstuffs according to their effect on the body is the basis in order to achieve a harmonious status of health.

Dietary advisors do not recommend certain foodstuffs for everyone. The individual diet is tailor-made for the individual constitution.

Buy only fresh and ripe fruit and vegetables. You ought to leave unripe fruit and vegetables and such with brown spots and wilted leaves behind in the market. In this case take deep-frozen goods (never ready-to-serve dishes!). Fruit and vegetables are deep-frozen immediately after harvesting and often contain more vitamins and minerals than the goods from the vegetable shelf. Whereas conserved or tinned goods contain very much less biological substances. Also, salt, sugar and others are mostly added to the latter. Never leave the foodstuffs in the water after washing them to avoid that many vital substances get drowned. Clean salads, fruit and vegetables immediately before serving.

Please make sure of the hygienic processing of foodstuffs. Clean your salads, fruit and vegetables carefully. When cooking with meat, prepare all ingredients first and then process the meat products. Clean the worktop and tools very carefully. Wooden surfaces ought to be treated with a mild disinfectant regularly in order to reduce germination.

Store fruit and vegetables separately, if possible. Harvested fruit and vegetables are still alive and emit e.g. ethylene gas, which makes other products ripen and age faster. Keep meat and fish in the closed packaging or store them in the fridge in closed containers.

12.4 Herbs

There are some basic rules for storing medicinal herbs. On principle, herbs must be protected from direct sunlight, humidity and heat.

Containers for the storage of herbs may be glasses, ceramic jars and even plastic containers. However, plastic is a rather unsuitable material and should only be a short-term solution. In case of glass containers, use a dark material.

Medicinal herbs cannot be kept for any long period. The shelf life of herbs is limited. However, it can be prolonged with suitable storage. The place should be dark, rather cool and absolutely dry. A wooden medicine cabinet, placed not directly next to a source of heat, would be ideal. Never buy large quantities of herbs so as not to have to throw them away. Label the container with the name of the herb and the date of harvesting or processing.

13 Other dietic-books

The following syndromes of dietetics, TCM or for a therapy supplement for cancer are available.

Dietetics

E001. Nutrition of the infant - baby food
E002. Nutrition during lactation
E003. Nutrition in old age
E004. Nutrition of children and adolescents
E005. Nutrition of athletes
E006. Light weight
E007. Pregnancy
E008. Full food

Protein and electrolyte - kidneys
E009. (hemodialysis) dialysis treatment
E010. Acute renal failure
E011. Chronic renal insufficiency
E012. Nephrotic syndrome
E013. Kidney stones (nephrolithiasis)

Gastrointestinal tract - pancreas
E014. Acute pancreatitis (inflammation of the pancreas)
E015. Chronic pancreatitis (inflammation of the pancreas)

Gastrointestinal tract - small intestine and large intestine
E016. Acute obstipation (constipation)
E017. Chronic obstipation (constipation)
E018. Colon irritabile
E019. Diverticulitis
E020. Acquired lactose intolerance (lactose malabsorption)
E021. Fructose malabsorption
E022. Glutensensitive enteropathy (celiac disease)
E023. Colectomy
E024. Short Bowel Syndrome

Gastrointestinal tract - liver, gallbladder, bile ducts
E025. Acute and chronic hepatitis (inflammation of the liver)
E026. Cholelithiasis (bile stones)
E027. fatty liver
E028. cirrhosis

Gastrointestinal tract - Stomach and duodenal intestine
E029. Acute gastritis
E030. Chronic gastritis
E031. Stomach bleeding
E032. Ulcus ventriculi and duodenal ulcer
E033. Condition after gastric surgery

Gastrointestinal tract - oral cavity and esophagus
E034. Stomatitis
E035. Esophageal carcinoma (esophageal cancer)
E036. Refluosophagitis (heartburn)

Special diseases
E037. Phenylketonuria (PKU)
E038. Rheumatic joint diseases

Metabolism
E039. Obesity (overweight)
E040. Diabetes mellitus
E041. Eating disorders (underweight)

Fat metabolism
E042. Hypercholesterolaemia (increased cholesterol level)
E043. Hepatic Encephalopathy

Heart and circulation
E044. Arteriosclerosis (arterial calcification)
E045. Heart insufficiency
E046. Hypertension
E047. Hyperuricaemia and gout

Changed nutrient requirements
E048. In case of fever
E049. For malignant diseases
E050. After burns
E051. Radiation and chemotherapy

CANCER
E100. Pancreatic cancer
E101. Bladder cancer
E102. Blood cancer (leukemia)
E103. Breast cancer
E104. Colorectal cancer
E105. Gastric cancer
E106. Kidney cancer
E107. Esophageal cancer

TCM
E200. Bladder - moisture heat in the bladder
E201. Bladder - moisture and cold in the bladder
E202. Bladder - emptiness and cold in the bladder
E203. Large intestine - external cold affects the large intestine
E204. Large intestine - moisture heat in the large intestine
E205. Large intestine - heat blocks the intestine II acute
E206. Large intestine - dryness of the colon
E207. Large intestine - Yang deficiency (cold)
E208. Heart - Blood insufficiency
E209. Heart - Blood stagnation
E210. Heart - Fire
E211. Heart - Hot mucus clogs the heart pores

E212. Heart - Cold mucus clogs the heart pores
E213. Heart - Qi deficiency
E214. Heart - Yang deficiency
E215. Heart - Yin deficiency
E216. Liver - Ascending Liver Yang
E217. Liver - Blood deficiency
E218. Liver - Blood stagnation
E219. Liver - Moisture heat in liver and gall bladder
E220. Liver - Fire
E221. Liver - Gall bladder Qi-Empty
E222. Liver - Cold in the liver meridian
E223. Liver - Qi stagnation
E224. Liver - Wind
E225. Liver - Wind with ascending liver Yang
E226. Liver - Wind with blood anemic
E227. Liver - Wind with extreme heat
E228. Lung - Qi deficiency
E229. Lung - Mucus-moisture in the lungs
E230. Lung - Mucus-heat in the lungs
E231. Lung - Mucus-cold in the lungs
E232. Lung - Dryness of the lungs
E233. Lung - Wind-heat attacks the lungs
E234. Lung - Wind-cold affects the lungs
E235. Lung - Yin deficiency
E236. Stomach - Bloodstagnation
E237. Stomach - Fire
E238. Stomach - Cold with liquid
E239. Stomach - Nutrition stagnation
E240. Stomach - Qi deficiency
E241. Stomach - Rebellious Qi
E242. Stomach - Yin Emptiness
E243. Spleen - Heat and moisture attack the spleen
E244. Spleen - Coldness and moisture affects the spleen
E245. Spleen - Qi deficiency
E246. Spleen - Qi deficiency + Declining spleen Qi
E247. Spleen - Qi deficiency + spleen does not control the blood
E248. Spleen - Yang deficiency
E249. Kidney - Heart and kidney no longer communicate
E250. Kidney - Jing deficiency
E251. Kidney - Kidneys cannot receive the Qi
E252. Kidney - Qi is not stable
E253. Kidney - Yang deficiency
E254. Kidney - Yin deficiency

For further information visit di-book.com.